Latin American Play Index

Volume 1: 1920-1962

by

HERBERT H. HOFFMAN

The Scarecrow Press, Inc.
Metuchen, N.J., and London
1984

Also by Herbert H. Hoffman:

Latin American Play Index, Volume 2: 1962-1980 (Scarecrow
    Press, 1983)
Cuento Mexicano Index (Headway Publications, 1978)

With Rita L. Hoffman:
International Index to Recorded Poetry (H. W. Wilson, 1983)

Library of Congress Cataloging in Publication Data
(Revised for volume 1)

Hoffman, Herbert H.
    Latin American play index.

    Contents: v. 1. 1920-1962 -- v. 2. 1962-1980.
    1. Latin American drama--Indexes. 2. Latin
American drama--Bibliography. I. Title.
Z1609.D7'H63   1984   016.862'008'098   83-8736
[PQ082.D7]
ISBN 0-8108-1671-7

Table of Contents

Foreword

In the four decades since 1920 more than 2000 plays have been published in South America as separate publications ("stand-alone works") or as contributions to collections, anthologies, and periodicals. Those included in Latin American Play Index, Volume 1: 1920-1962, were written by some 600 playwrights in Spanish, Portuguese, and French. In combination with Latin American Play Index, Volume 2: 1962-1980, therefore, access is provided to about 3300 South American plays published between 1920 and 1980, by some 1000 authors.

Latin American Play Index covers plays published in four formats. Some appeared as stand-alone works; others were published in collections (defined as books containing several plays by the same author); still others were published in anthologies (defined as books containing plays by different authors); a limited number were published in periodicals.

The majority of the collections and anthologies covered in Volume 1 appear in the well-known Handbook of Latin American Studies (HLAS), and for this reason the HLAS volume and entry numbers have been adopted as reference codes. Only those books coded "0" do not appear in HLAS. The complete List of Collections and Anthologies begins on page 130.

For the sake of standardization, Latin American Play Index has adopted, whenever possible, the same periodical codes that were introduced by HLAS. Thus, the code UCCH/A stands for the periodical Apuntes of Santiago de Chile. The List of Periodicals Indexed begins on page 144.

Stand-alone plays are described by author, title, and imprint. Throughout, HLAS volume and entry numbers have been added so that readers may easily refer to relevant critical notes and other useful information found in that handbook.

Herbert H. Hoffman

ERRATA

Volume 2:

Page 62--Ponferrada is the correct spelling

Page 75--add the following entries:

Tavares, Severino M.
Hoje a banda não sai. In anthol. 42/6381

Telles, C. Q.
Ultima instância. In anthol. 42/6366

Téllez, L.
Tercera ley de Newton, La. In anthol. 38/7161

Tenorio, M. A.
Paletero tenía la razón, El. In anthol. 38/7161

Thomas, José de
Lobo en la ciudad, El. (Buenos Aires : Ediciones del Carro de Tespis, 1967 ; 30/3934)

Tobar García, Francisco.
Cuando el mar no exista. In col. 32/4487
Dama ciega, La. In coll. 32/4487
En los ojos vacíos de la gente. In anthol. 38/7196

Page 114--correct date in entry 30/3887 to 1967

Playwrights Included

[Names preceded by an * are also represented in Volume 2.]

Abreu Gomez, Ermilo. 1894.
Mexico.
Abreu, Modesto de. 1901.
Brazil.
Abreu, Nelson de. Brazil.
Accioly Netto, Antonio. 1906.
Brazil.
*Acevedo Hernández, Antonio.
1886. Chile.
Acuña, Juan Enrique. 1915.
Argentina.
Acuña, Manuel. 1849. Mex-
ico.
*Aguilera Malta, Demetrio.
1909. Ecuador.
*Aguirre, Isidora. 1919.
Chile.
Aguirre, Manuel Alberto.
Alberdi, Juan Bautista. 1810.
Argentina.
Alencar, José Martiniano de.
1829. Brazil.
Alfonso, Paco (Francisco Al-
fonso Hernandez). Cuba.
Algarra, María Luisa. Mex-
ico.
*Aliber, Alicia. Argentina.
Aliber, Bernardo. Argentina.
*Almeida, Abílio Pereira de.
1906. Brazil.
Alsina, José Arturo. 1897.
Paraguay.
Alvarez Lleras, Antonio.
1892. Colombia.

Alvarez Ríos, María. Cuba.
Alvim, Renato. 1890.
Brazil.
Amado, Genolino. 1903.
Brazil.
*Amado, João Jorge. 1912.
Brazil.
Amador, Graciela. Mexico.
Amorim, Enrique. 1900.
Uruguay.
Anaya-Sarmiento, Héctor.
Mexico.
*Anchieta, José de. 1534.
Brazil.
Ancira, Carlos. Mexico.
*Andrade, Jorge. Brazil.
Angulo y Guridi, Javier.
1816. Dominican Re-
public.
Aquino, Pedro Benjamín.
1887. Argentina.
*Arango, Gonzalo. 1930.
Colombia.
*Araújo, Nelson Correia de.
1926. Brazil.
*Arauz, Alvaro. Mexico.
*Argüelles, Hugo. 1932.
Mexico.
*Arreola, Juan José. 1918.
Mexico.
Arriola Ledesma, Abelardo.
Peru.
*Arriví, Francisco. 1915.
Puerto Rico.

- 1 -

*Arrufat, Antón. 1935. Cuba.
*Asturias, Miguel Angel. 1899.
    Guatemala.
Asúnsolo, Enrique. Mexico.
*Avilés Blonda, Máximo. 1931.
    Dominican Republic.
Ayala Michelena, Leopoldo.
    Venezuela.
*Azar, Héctor. 1930. Mex-
    ico.
Azevedo, Aluisio. 1857.
    Brazil.
*Azevedo, Arthur. 1855.
    Brazil.
Azuela, Mariano. 1873.
    Mexico.
*Badía, Nora. 1921. Cuba.
*Báez, Edmundo. 1914. Mex-
    ico.
*Balla, Andrés. Argentina.
Baralt, Luis Alejandro. 1892.
    Cuba.
Barbieri, Vicente. 1903.
    Argentina.
Barreiro, José. Cuba.
*Barreto, Paulo. 1878.
    Brazil.
*Barros Grez, Daniel. 1834.
    Chile.
*Basurto, Luis G. 1920.
    Mexico.
Bayon Herrera, Luis. Ar-
    gentina.
Beccaglia, Juan María. Ar-
    gentina.
*Belaval, Emilio S. 1903.
    Puerto Rico.
Bellán, José Pedro. 1889.
    Uruguay.
Bellini, Mario. Argentina.
Benedetti, Lúcia. 1914.
    Brazil.
*Benedetti, Mario. 1920.
    Uruguay.
*Béneke, Walter. 1928. El
    Salvador.

Bengoa, Juan León. 1895.
    Uruguay.
Bernal, Rafael. Mexico.
*Berruti, Alejandro E. Ar-
    gentina.
Bettencourt, Carlos. Bra-
    zil.
*Betti, Atilio. 1922. Ar-
    gentina.
*Bioy Casares, Adolfo.
    1914. Argentina.
Blanco-Amor, Eduardo.
    1900. Argentina.
Blest Gana, Alberto. 1830.
    Chile.
*Bloch, Pedro. 1914.
    Brazil.
*Bocanegra, Matías de.
    1612. Mexico.
Bocayuva, Quintino. 1836.
    Brazil.
Bofanini, Darcília Azarany.
    Brazil.
Bollo, Sarah. Uruguay.
*Borba Filho, Hermilo.
    1917. Brazil.
Borges, Jorge Luis. 1894.
    Argentina.
*Borges, José Carlos
    Cavalcânti. Brazil.
Borrás, Eduardo. Argen-
    tina.
Boscoli, Geysa. 1907.
    Brazil.
Bourbakis, Roberto. Cuba.
Brau, Salvador. 1842.
    Puerto Rico.
Bravo Garzón, Roberto.
    Mexico.
Bressan, Alma. Argentina.
Brierre, Jean Fernand.
    1909. Haiti.
Brook, Paulita. Mexico.
Bruno, Jorge. Uruguay.
Bruno, Pedro Mariano.
    Argentina.

Buch, René A. Cuba.
*Buenaventura, Enrique. 1925.
Colombia.
Buffo, Guido. Argentina.
Buitrago, Fanny. 1944.
Colombia.
*Bustillo Oro, Juan. 1904.
Mexico.
*Buttaro, Enrique. Argentina.
Caldera, Daniel. Chile.
Calderón, Fernando. 1809.
Mexico.
*Callado, Antônio. Brazil.
Calvente de Helmbold, Ana
María. Argentina.
Calvillo Madrigal, Salvador.
Mexico.
Camargo, Christovão de.
1902. Brazil.
*Camargo, Joracy. 1898.
Brazil.
Cambours Ocampo, Arturo.
Argentina.
Campos, Eduardo. 1923.
Brazil.
*Campos, Geir. 1924. Bra-
zil.
Canal-Feijóo, Bernardo.
1897. Argentina.
*Cañas, Alberto. 1920.
Costa Rica.
*Cantón, Wilberto. 1923.
Mexico.
Capablanca, Enrique G. de.
Cuba.
Capdevila, Arturo. 1889.
Argentina.
Caraco, Alberto. Brazil.
*Carballido, Emilio. 1925.
Mexico.
Carballo de Núñez, Carlota.
Peru.
*Cardoso, Lúcio. 1913. Bra-
zil.
*Cardozo, Joaquim. 1897.
Brazil.

Cariola Villagrán, Carlos.
1895. Chile.
*Carlino, Carlos. 1910.
Argentina.
Carneiro, Nelson. Brazil.
Carvalho, Afonso de. 1897.
Brazil.
Carvalho, Fernando Livino
de. Brazil.
Casas, Myrna. Puerto
Rico.
Castillero Reyes, Ernesto
de Jesús. 1889.
Panama.
*Castillo, Abelardo. 1935.
Argentina.
Castillo de González,
Aurelio. 1842. Cuba.
Castillo F., Ricardo. Co-
lombia.
Castorena, José de Jesús.
1901. Mexico.
Castro Saavedra, Carlos.
Colombia.
Catani, Enrique. 1914.
Argentina.
Catania, Carlos. Costa
Rica.
Cayol, Roberto Lino. 1887.
Argentina.
Cecco, Sergio Amadeo de.
1931. Argentina.
Centurión Miranda, R.
Paraguay.
Cepelos, Batista. 1872.
Brazil.
Certad, Aquiles. 1914.
Venezuela.
Cervantes, Dagoberto de.
Mexico.
*Césaire, Aimé. Martinique.
Chacón. Cuba.
*Chalbaud, Román. 1931.
Venezuela.
Chesta Aránguiz, José.
Chile.

Chioino, José. 1878. Peru.
*Chocrón, Isaac. 1932. Venezuela.
*Cid Pérez, José. 1906. Cuba.
Coelho Netto, Paulo. 1902. Brazil.
Cogolani, Roberto Dante. Argentina.
Conrado, Aldomar. Brazil.
Córdoba Romero, Guillermo. Colombia.
Cordone, Rogelio. Argentina.
Córdova, Luis. 1908. Mexico.
*Coronel Urtecho, José. 1906. Nicaragua.
Correa, Julio. Paraguay.
Correa, Pancho (Americo Tabárez). Uruguay.
*Corrêa, Viriato. 1883. Brazil.
Cortinas, Ismael. 1884. Uruguay.
*Cossa, Roberto M. 1934. Argentina.
Costantini, Humberto. 1924. Argentina.
Crimi, Humberto. Argentina.
*Cruz, Sor Juana Inés de la. 1648. Mexico.
*Cuadra, Pablo Antonio. 1912. Nicaragua.
Cunha, Humberto. Brazil.
*Cuzzani, Agustín. 1924. Argentina.
Dantas, Raymundo Souza. 1923. Brazil.
Dauphin, Marcel. Haiti.
Dávalos, Juan Carlos. 1887. Argentina.
Dávalos, Marcelino. 1871. Mexico.
Daycard, Enriqueta. Chile.

*Debesa, Fernando. 1921. Chile.
*Defilippis Novoa, Francisco. 1892. Argentina.
*Denevi, Marco. 1922. Argentina.
D'Erzell, Catalina. Mexico.
De Stefani, Alejandro. Argentina.
Deugenio, Rubén. 1925. Uruguay.
*Díaz Díaz, Oswaldo. Colombia.
*Díaz Dufóo, Carlos. 1861. Mexico.
*Díaz González, Olallo. Cuba.
*Díaz, Jorge. 1930. Argentina.
Díaz Sánchez, Ramón. 1903. Venezuela.
Díez Barroso, Victor Manuel. 1890. Mexico.
*Discépolo, Armando. 1887. Argentina.
*Discépolo, Enrique Santos. 1901. Argentina.
Doblas, Raúl. Argentina.
*Domingos, Anselmo. Brazil.
Domínguez, Franklin. 1931. Dominican Republic.
Domínguez, Pablo. 1901. Venezuela.
Dow, Alberto. Colombia.
Dracco-Bracco, Adolfo. Guatemala.
*Dragún, Osvaldo. 1929. Argentina.
Ducasse, Vendenesse. Haiti.
*Eichelbaum, Samuel. 1894. Argentina.
Eiró, Paulo. 1836. Brazil.

Elorduy, Aquiles. 1875.
Mexico.
Epiñeira, Antonio. Chile.
Ercilla, Alonso de. 1569.
Chile.
Ernhard, James
(Camilo Pérez de Arce).
Chile.
Espejo, Beatriz. Mexico.
*Estorino, Abelardo. 1925.
Cuba.
Estrada, Ricardo. Guatemala.
Fabiani, Víctor. Argentina.
Fabregat Cúneo, Roberto.
1906. Uruguay.
Faria, Octávio de. 1908.
Brazil.
Faro, Arnaldo. Brazil.
Feder, Carlos Eduardo.
Argentina.
Feijóo, Samuel. 1914.
Cuba.
Fein, María Teresa.
Uruguay.
*Felipe, Carlos. 1914. Cuba.
*Fernandes, Millôr. 1923.
Brazil
Fernandes, Nabor. Brazil.
*Fernández de Lizardi,
José Joaquín. 1776.
Mexico.
Fernández, Piri. Puerto Rico.
Fernández Suárez, Alvaro.
Uruguay.
Fernández Unsain, José María.
1918. Argentina.
*Ferrari Amores, Alfonso.
1903. Argentina.
*Ferrer, Rolando. 1925.
Cuba.
*Ferretti, Aurelio. 1907.
Argentina.
*Figueiredo, Guilherme de.
1915. Brazil.
Flores Chinarro, Francisco.
1838. Peru.
*Florit, Eugenio. 1903.
Cuba.

Folino, Norberto.
Argentina.
Fonseca, José Paulo M.
da. 1922. Brazil.
Fontoura, Matheus da.
1899. Brazil.
Fornari, Ernani. 1899.
Brazil.
Fornés, María Irene.
Cuba.
Fortes, Betty Yelda
Brognoli Borges.
Brazil.
*França Júnior,
Joaquim José da.
1838. Brazil.
Franco, Afonso Arinos
de Melo. 1905.
Brazil.
Freire Júnior, F. J.
Brazil.
Fuente, Sindulfo de la.
Mexico.
*Galich, Manuel. 1912.
Guatemala.
Gallegos, Gerardo. Mexico.
Gallegos, Rómulo. Vene-
zuela.
Galli, Santiago. Argen-
tina.
Gallo, Blas Raúl. Argen-
tina.
Gama, Jota. Brazil.
Gamarra, Abelardo M.
1850. Peru.
Gamboa, Federico.
1864. Mexico.
Gamboa, José Joaquin.
1878. Mexico.
García Berlanga, Luis.
Uruguay.
García de Paredes,
Carlos M. Panama.
García, Juan Agustín.
1862. Argentina.
*García Ponce, Juan.
1932. Mexico.

*García Velloso, Enrique.
  1880. Argentina.
*Garro, Elena. 1922. Mexico.
Gavidia, Francisco Antonio.
  1864. El Salvador.
Gené, Juan Carlos. 1928.
  Argentina.
Genta, Walter Homero.
  Argentina.
*Ghiano, Juan Carlos. 1920.
  Argentina.
Ghiraldo, Alberto. 1874.
  Argentina.
Gibson Parra, Percy. Peru.
Girbal, Gladys Teresa.
  Argentina.
Girón Cerna, Carlos.
  Guatemala.
Godoy, Emma. Mexico.
Goicochea, Carlos.
  Argentina.
Golwarz, Sergio. Mexico.
*Gomes Dias, Alfredo. 1914.
  Brazil.
*Gomes, Roberto. 1882.
  Brazil.
Gonçalves Dias, Antônio.
  1823. Brazil.
*Gondim Filho, Isaac.
  Brazil.
Gonzaga, Armando. 1889.
  Brazil.
González Arrili, Bernardo.
  1892. Argentina.
*González Castillo, José.
  1885. Argentina.
*González de Eslava, Fernán
  1534. Mexico.
González, Ingrid. Cuba.
González Pacheco, Rodolfo.
  1881. Argentina.
González Paredes, Ramón.
  Venezuela.
*Gorostiza, Carlos, 1920.
  Argentina.
*Gorostiza, Celestino. 1904.
  Mexico.

*Gorostiza, Manuel
  Eduardo de. 1789.
  Mexico.
Gramcko, Ida. Venezuela.
*Guarnieri, Gianfrancesco.
  1934. Brazil.
Guillén, Nicolás. 1902.
  Cuba.
Guimarães, Antonio.
  Brazil.
Guimarães, Pinheiro.
  1832. Brazil.
Guizado, Rafael. Colombia.
Gurgel, Amaral. Brazil.
*Gutiérrez, Eduardo. 1853.
  Argentina.
Gutiérrez Hermosillo,
  Alfonso. 1905.
  Mexico.
Guzmán Cruchaga, Juan.
  1896. El Salvador.
Harmony, Olga. Mexico.
*Heiremans, Luis Alberto.
  1928. Chile.
Hernández, Fausto.
  Argentina.
Hernández, Leopoldo.
  Cuba.
*Hernández, Luisa Josefina.
  1928. Mexico.
*Herrera, Ernesto. 1886.
  Uruguay.
Herrera y Reissig, Julio.
  1875. Uruguay.
*Holanda, Nestor de. 1921.
  Brazil.
Ibarbourou, Juana de.
  1895. Uruguay.
*Ibargüengoitia, Jorge.
  1928. Mexico.
Icaza, Jorge. 1906.
  Ecuador.
Iglezias, Luiz. 1905.
  Brazil.
*Imbert, Julio. 1918.
  Argentina.
*Inclán, Federico S. 1910.
  Mexico.

Innes-Gonzáles, Eduardo.
1882. Venezuela.
Jaramillo Arango, Rafael.
Colombia.
Jardim, Luís Inácio de
Miranda. 1901. Brazil.
Jiménez, Miguel Angel.
Dominican Republic.
Jiménez Rueda, Julio. 1896.
Mexico.
Jiménez, Wilfredo. 1915.
Argentina.
Josseau, Fernando.
Argentina.
Kelly, Celso. 1906. Brazil.
*Kraly, Néstor. Argentina.
Krimer, Jorge. Argentina.
*Laferrère, Gregorio de. 1867.
Argentina.
Lago, Mario. Brazil.
Laguerre, Enrique A.
Puerto Rico.
*Larreta, Antonio. 1922.
Uruguay.
Larreta, Enrique Rodríguez.
1875. Argentina.
*Lasser, Alejandro. 1916.
Venezuela.
Lavardén, Manuel de. 1754.
Argentina.
Lazo, Agustín. 1879.
Mexico.
*Leguizamón, Martiniano.
1858. Argentina.
*Lehmann, Marta. Argentina.
Lermitte, Carlos. 1896.
Uruguay.
Lima, Benjamin. 1885.
Brazil.
*Lima, Edy. Brazil.
Lira, Miguel Nicolás. 1905.
Mexico.
List Arzubide, Germán. 1898.
Mexico.
*Lizárraga, Andrés. 1919.
Argentina.
Llanderas, Nicolás de las.
Argentina.

Lontiel, Octavio.
Argentina.
Lopes Cardoso, A.
Brazil.
López Crespo, Iris de.
Uruguay.
López Lorenzo, Manuel.
1842. Argentina.
Louzada, Armando.
Brazil.
Lozano García, Carlos.
Mexico.
Macau, Miguel Angel.
1886. Cuba.
*Macedo, Joaquim Manuel de.
1820. Brazil.
*Machado de Assis,
Joaquim Maria. 1839.
Brazil.
Machado, Lourival. 1917.
Brazil.
*Machado, Maria Clara.
Brazil.
Magalhães, Heloisa Helena.
Brazil.
*Magalhães Júnior, Raymundo.
1907. Brazil.
*Magalhães, Paulo de. 1900.
Brazil.
*Magaña, Sergio. 1924.
Mexico.
Magdaleno, Mauricio. 1906.
Mexico.
*Maggi, Carlos. 1922.
Uruguay.
*Malfatti, Arnaldo M.
Argentina.
Mallea, Eduardo. 1903.
Argentina.
Manceaux, Alberto.
Argentina.
Manco, Silveiro. Argentina.
Manet, Eduardo. Cuba.
*María, Enrique de. 1870.
Argentina.
*Marín, Gerard Paul.
Puerto Rico.
Marín, Juan. 1900.

*Marqués, René. 1919.
Puerto Rico.
*Martí, José. 1853. Cuba.
Martínez Cuitiño, Vicente.
1887. Argentina/
Uruguay.
Martínez Estrada, Ezequiel.
1895. Argentina.
*Martínez, José de Jesús.
1929. Nicaragua.
Masip, Paulino. 1899.
Mexico.
Matorras Cornejo, Carlos.
Argentina.
Maturana, José de. 1884.
Argentina.
*Medina, Roberto Nicolás.
Argentina.
Mediz Bolio, Antonio. 1884.
Mexico.
*Méndez Ballester, Manuel.
1905. Puerto Rico.
Mendoza Gutiérrez, Alfredo.
Mexico.
Mendoza, Héctor. 1932.
Mexico.
*Menéndez, Roberto Arturo.
1931. El Salvador.
Mesquita, Alfredo. 1907.
Brazil.
Messina, Felipe. Brazil.
Meyrialle, Horacio S.
Argentina.
*Milanés, José Jacinto. 1814.
Cuba.
Milanez, Abdon. Brazil.
Miró, César. Peru.
*Molleto, Enrique. 1922. Chile.
*Mombrú, María. Argentina.
Mondragón Aguirre, Magdalena.
1913. Mexico.
*Montaine, Eliseo. Argentina.
*Montalvo, Juan. 1832. Ecua-
dor.
*Monteiro, José Maria.
Brazil.
Montello, Josué. 1917.
Brazil.

Monterde, Francisco.
1894. Mexico.
Montero, Marco Antonio.
Mexico.
*Montes Huidobro, Matías de.
1931. Cuba.
Moock Bousquet, Armando.
1894. Chile.
*Mora, Juan Miguel de.
1840. Mexico.
Moraes, Marcus Vinicius
de Melo. Brazil.
Moreno, Gloria. Chile.
Moreno, Luis. Mexico.
Morisseau-Leroy, Félix.
1912. Haiti.
Mota, Fernando. Mexico.
*Nalé Roxlo, Conrado.
1898. Argentina.
Nascimento, Abdias do.
1914. Brazil.
Navarrete, Rodolfo. 1922.
Argentina.
*Neto, Coêlho (Henrique
Maximiano Coelho
Neto.) 1864. Brazil.
Noriega Hope, Carlos.
Mexico.
*Novión, Alberto. 1881.
Argentina.
*Novo, Salvador. 1904.
Mexico.
Nunes, Mario. Brazil.
Ocampo, María Luisa.
1905. Mexico.
Olivari, Carlos. Argentina.
Olivari, Nicolás. 1900.
Argentina.
Oliveira e Silva, Francisco.
1897. Brazil.
Oliveira, Jocy de. Brazil.
*Oliveira, Valdemar de.
Brazil.
Olmedo López, Eduardo.
Bolivia.
Ordóñez, Eduardo. Cuba.
Orgambide, Pedro G. 1929.
Argentina.

Orlando, Paulo. Brazil.
Orosa Díaz, Jaime. Mexico.
Orrego Vicuña, Eugenio. 1900.
  Chile.
Orteiza, Alberto M.
  Argentina.
Ortíz de Montellano, Bernardo.
  1899. Mexico.
Ortiz Guerrero, Manuel.
  Paraguay.
*Osorio, Luis Enrique.
  Colombia.
Othón, Manuel José. 1858.
  Mexico.
Ozores, Renato. Panama.
*Pacheco, Carlos Mauricio.
  1881. Argentina.
Páez, Leonardo. Ecuador.
*Pagano, José León. 1875.
  Argentina.
Pagés Larraya, Antonio.
  Argentina.
*Palant, Pablo. 1914.
  Argentina.
Palino, Piquio. Argentina.
Paolantonio, Jorge M.
  Argentina.
*Paoli, Carlos de. Argentina.
Parada León, Ricardo.
  Mexico.
Paredes, Margarita V. de.
  Dominican Republic.
*Parrado, Gloria. Cuba.
*Pasos, Joaquin. 1915.
  Nicaragua.
Patrón, Juan Carlos.
  Argentina.
*Payró, Roberto J. 1867.
  Argentina.
*Paz, Octavio. 1914.
Pederneiras, Raul. 1874.
  Brazil.
Peixoto, Luiz. Brazil.
Peixoto, Maria Luiza Amaral.
  Brazil.
Pellgrini, Aldo. 1903.
  Argentina.

Penna, Luíz Carlos Martins.
  1815. Brazil.
*Peón y Contreras, José.
  1843. Mexico.
Pereña, Alfredo. Mexico.
Pérez Pardella, Agustín.
  Argentina.
Pérez Taylor, Rafael.
  1890. Mexico.
Perrín, Tomás. Mexico.
Pico, Pedro E. 1882.
  Argentina.
*Piñera, Virgilio. 1912.
  Cuba.
Pitol, Sergio. 1933.
  Mexico.
Piza, José. Brazil.
*Plá, Josefina. 1909.
  Paraguay.
Planchart, Julio. Vene-
  zuela
Planchart, María Luisa de.
  Venezuela.
Plaza, Angélica. Uruguay.
Plaza Noblía, Héctor.
  Uruguay.
Podestá, José. Argentina.
Pondal Ríos, Sixto.
  1907. Argentina.
*Ponferrada, Juan Oscar.
  1908. Argentina.
*Pongetti, Henrique. 1898.
  Brazil.
Porto, Miguel Antonio.
  1862. Cuba.
Potts, Renée. Cuba.
Prieto, Carlos. 1922.
  Mexico.
Princivalle, Carlos Maria.
  Uruguay.
*Queiroz, Rachel de. 1910.
  Brazil.
Ramirez M. , José. 1916.
  Mexico.
Ramos, José Antonio.
  1885. Cuba.
Rapoport, Nicolás, Ar-
  gentina.

Rebêlo, Marques (Eddy Dias
    da Cruz.) 1907.
    Brazil.
*Rechani Agrait, Luis.
    Puerto Rico.
Rega Molina, Horacio. 1899.
    Argentina.
*Reguera Saumell, Manuel.
    1928. Cuba.
Rendón, Victor Manuel.
    1859. Ecuador.
*Rengifo, César. 1915.
    Venezuela.
*Requena, María Asuncion.
    1918. Chile.
*Retes, Ignacio. 1918.
    Mexico.
Reyes, Alfonso. 1889.
    Mexico.
*Rial, Jose Antonio.
    Venezuela.
Ríos, Juan. Peru.
Rivera Alvarez, Edmundo.
    Puerto Rico.
*Robles, J. Humberto. 1921.
    Mexico.
Roca Rey, Bernardo. Peru.
Rocha, Aurimar. Brazil.
Rocha, Daniel. 1908. Brazil.
Rodrigues, Ferreira. Brazil.
*Rodrigues, Nelson. 1912.
    Brazil.
Rodríguez, Franklin.
*Rodríguez Galván, Ignacio.
    1816. Mexico.
Rodríguez, Yamandú. 1895.
    Argentina.
*Roepke, Gabriela. 1920.
    Chile.
Rojas, Ricardo. 1882.
    Argentina.
Romero de Terreros y Vinent,
    Manuel. 1880. Mexico.
Romero Peláez, Celso.
    Chile.
*Rosencof, Mauricio. 1934.
    Uruguay.
Rosenrauch, E. Chile.

Rubertino, María Luisa.
    1923. Argentina.
Ruiz Aldea, Pedro. 1835.
    Chile.
Ruiz, Raúl. Chile.
Sábat Ercasty, Carlos.
    1887. Uruguay.
Sábato, Ernesto. 1911.
    Argentina.
Sabido, Miguel. Mexico.
Sada Hermosillo, Concep-
    ción. Mexico.
*Sáenz, Dalmiro. 1926.
    Argentina.
*Salazar Bondy, Sebastián.
    1924. Peru.
Saldías, José Antonio.
    1891. Argentina.
Salgado, Antoine. Haiti.
Salinas, Marcelo. 1889.
    Cuba.
Salinas Pérez, Pablo.
    Mexico.
*Sampaio, José da Silveira.
    1914. Brazil.
Sampaio, Moreira. Brazil.
*Sánchez, Florencio. 1875.
    Uruguay/Argentina.
Sánchez Galarraga, Gustavo.
    1892. Cuba.
Sánchez Gardel, Julio.
    1879. Argentina.
*Sánchez, Luis Rafael.
    1936. Puerto Rico.
Sánchez Maldonado,
    Benjamín. Cuba.
*Sánchez Mayans, Fernando.
    Mexico.
Sánchez Varona, Ramón.
    1883. Cuba.
Sancho, Alfredo.
    El Salvador.
*Sándor, Malena. Argentina.
Santander, Felipe. Mexico.
Santibañes, César de.
    Argentina.
Santos, Justino. Brazil.
Santos, Miguel. 1884.
    Brazil.

Saráh Comandari, Roberto
(Andres Terbay.)   1916.
Chile.
Sarobe, Angélica.   Argentina.
Schaefer Gallo, Carlos.   1890.
Argentina.
Schroeder Inclán, Federico.
1910.   Mexico.
Segovia, Tomás.   1927.
Mexico.
*Segura, Manuel Ascensio.
1805.   Peru.
Seljan, Zora.   Brazil.
Seoane, Luis.   1910.   Argen-
Argentina.
Sepúlveda Iriondo, Ariel.
tina.
Sierra Berdecía, Fernando.
Puerto Rico.
Sierra, Justo.   1848.   Mexico.
*Sieveking, Alejandro.   1934.
Chile.
Silberstein, Enrique.   Argentina.
Silva, Antônio José da.   1705.
Brazil.
Silva Gutiérrez, Jaime.   Chile.
Silva Valdés, Fernán.   1887.
Uruguay.
Silvain, Julio César.   1926.
Argentina.
Silveira, Helena.   1911.   Brazil.
Soferman, Arturo.   Uruguay.
*Solana, Rafael.   1915.   Mexico.
*Solari Swayne, Enrique.   Peru.
Solly (Solly Wolodarsky.)   Ar-
gentina.
*Solórzano, Carlos.   1922.
Guatemala.
Sotoconil, Rubén.   Chile.
Sousa, Afonso Felix de.   1925.
Brazil.
*Souto, Alexandrino de.
Brazil.
Souza, Antonio.   1928.   Mex-
ico.
Spota, Luis.   Mexico.
*Steiner, Rolando.   1936.
Nicaragua.

*Suassuna, Ariano.   1927.
Brazil.
Subercaseaux, Benjamín.
1902.   Chile.
*Tálice, Roberto Alejandro.
1902.   Argentina.
Tarruella, Víctor.   Chile.
Testena, Folco.   Argentina.
*Thomas, José de.   Argen-
tina.
Tigre, Manoel Bastos.
1882.   Brazil.
Tinoco, Godofredo.
Brazil.
*Tojeiro, Gastão.   1880.
Brazil.
Torres Chaves, Efraín.
Ecuador.
*Tourinho, Nazareno.
Brazil.
Trejo, Mario.   1926.
Argentina.
*Trejo, Nemesio.   1862.
Argentina.
*Triana, José.   1933.
Cuba.
Trovão da Costa,
Maria Jacintha.
Brazil.
Trovão de Campos,
Maria Jacinta.
Brazil.
Uhthoff, Enrique.   Mexico.
Urueta, Margarita.   1918.
Mexico.
*Usigli, Rodolfo.   1905.
Mexico.
Uslar-Pietri, Arturo.
1906.   Venezuela.
*Vacarezza, Alberto.   1896.
Argentina.
Valencia, Gerardo.   Co-
lombia.
Vanasco, Alberto.   1925.
Argentina.
Vanicóre, Clóris.
Brazil.

Vargas Tejada, Luis. 1802.
   Colombia.
Velarde, Héctor. Peru.
Vera, Pedro Jorge. 1914.
   Ecuador.
*Vianna Filho, Oduvaldo (also
   Viana, O. and Viana,
   Oduvaldo.) 1936.
   Brazil.
*Vianna, Oduvaldo (also Viana,
   Oduvaldo.) 1892.
   Brazil.
Vianna, Renato (also Viana).
   1894. Brazil.
*Vilalta, Maruxa. 1932.
   Mexico.
*Villaurrutia, Xavier. 1903.
   Mexico.
Villegas Vidal, Juan Carlos.
   Argentina.
Vitor, Léo. Brazil.

*Vodánovic, Sergio. 1928.
   Chile.
Wainer, Alberto. Argentina.
*Wanderley, José. 1905.
   Brazil.
Wanderley Menezes, Maria.
   Brazil.
Weisbach, Alberto T. 1883.
   Argentina.
Wiesse, María. 1894. Peru.
*Wolff, Egon. 1926. Chile.
X. Cuba.
Young, Juan Raul. Argentina.
Yunque, Alvaro (Arístides
   Gandolfi Herrero.)
   1890. Argentina.
Zavalía, Alberto de. 1911.
   Argentina.
Zavattini, Cesare. 1902.
   Uruguay.
Zendejas, Francisco. 1919.
   Mexico.

Author Index: Sample Entries

Mendoza, Hector.
      Camelia, La.   In per. UNAM/UM, 13:10, jun. '59, p.
         13-15 (23/5333)
      Cosas simples, Las.   (Mexico : Libreria Studium, 1954;
         19/5166); also in anthol. 20/4234.

Explanation.

     The first, "La Camelia," was published in the period-
ical Universidad de México (code UNAM/UM) for June 1959,
on pages 13-15.   An annotation can be found in the Handbook
of Latin American Studies, volume 23, under entry number
5333.

     The second, "Las cosas simples," is a separately pub-
lished play, a stand-alone work.   It was published in Mexico
in 1954 and an annotation can be found in the Handbook of
Latin American Studies, volume 19, under entry number 5166.
The same play was also included in an anthology.   The complete bibliographic description of the anthology can be found
under code number 20/4234 in the List of Collections and Anthologies (page 130).   A brief note about the play can be
found in the Handbook of Latin American Studies, volume 20,
under entry number 4234.

Author Index

[Names preceded by an * are also represented in Volume 2]

Abreu Gómez, Ermilo.
    Humanidades. (México : Impr. del Comercio, 1923)
    Romance de reyes. (Madrid : Espasa-Calpe, 1926)
    Un loro y tres golondrinas. (México : Letras de Méx-
        ico, 194?; 14/2948); also in per. HIJO PRODIGO,
        año 3, v. 9, n. 28, julio 1945, p. 34-44 (11/3325)
    Viva el rey. (México : Impr. del Comercio, 1921)

Abreu, Modesto de.
    Ermitão da gloria, O. (Rio : Papeleria e tip. Coelho,
        1943; 9/4295)
    Quando o coração quer.... In per. RTB, n. 277, j/f
        '54.

Abreu, Nelson de, jt. auth. see under Alvim, Renato.

Accioly Netto, Antonio.
    Helena fechou a porta. In coll. 20/4418.
    Mentira de cada dia, A. In coll. 20/4418.
    Vida não é nossa, A. In coll. 4418.

*Acevedo Hernández, Antonio.
    18 típico, Un. (Santiago : Nascimento, 1929); also in
        coll. 0/13.
    Almas perdidas. (4th ed. Santiago : Nascimento, 1932);
        also in coll. 0/14.
    Angélica. (Santiago : Nascimento, 1933); also in coll.
        0/14.
    Arbol viejo. (Santiago : Nascimento, 1934); also in
        coll. 0/13.
    Cabrerita. (Santiago : Nascimento, 1929); in English
        under the same title in anthol. 0/80.
    Caín. (Santiago : Nascimento, 1927); also in coll. 0/13.
    Camino de flores. (Santiago : Nascimento, 1929); also
        in coll. 0/13.

Canción rota, La.   (Santiago : Nascimento, 1933); also
    in coll. 0/13.
Cardo negro.   (Santiago : Nascimento, 1933); also in
    coll. 0/13 and 0/14.
Chañarcillo.   In per. EXCELSIOR, año 1, n. 25, 1936,
    p. 32-66; also in anthol. 22/5315.
De pura cepa (Santiago : Nascimento, 1929); also in
    coll. 0/13.
Joaquín Murieta.   In per. EXCELSIOR, año 1, supl.
    1, 1936, p. 3-30.
Por el atajo.   (Santiago : Nascimento, 1932): also in
    coll. 0/13.
Qién quiere mi virtud!   (Santiago : Nascimento, 1929);
    also in coll. 0/13.
Triángulo tiene cuatro lados, El.   (Santiago : Ediciones
    A. Acevedo Hernandez, 1963; 28/2262)

Acuña, Juan Enrique.
    Ciudad condenada, La.   (Buenos Aires : Ariadna, 1957;
        21/4200)

Acuña, Manuel.
    Pasado, El.   In coll. 15/2434.

*Aguilera Malta, Demetrio.
    Dientes blancos.   In coll. 0/15 and 23/5300.
    Honorarios.   In coll. 23/5300.
    Lázaro.   (Guayaquil : Imp. del Colegio Vicente Roca-
        fuerte, 19?; 12/2745)
    No bastan los átomos.   In coll. 0/15.
    Sangre azul.   (Washington : Unión Panamericana, 1948;
        also published in Portuguese as Sangue azul;
        14/2949)
    Tigre, El.   In coll. 23/5300; also in anthol. 22/5315
        and 28/2388b.

*Aguirre, Isidora.
    Carolina.   In English as Express for Santiago in anthol.
        0/101.

Aguirre, Manuel Alberto.
    Ideas nuevas.   (Chiclayo, 1935?; 1/2109)

Alberdi, Juan Bautista.
    Revolución de Mayo, La.   (Buenos Aires : Imprenta de
        la Universidad, 1925; also Córdoba, Arg. : Univer-
        sidad Nacional de Córdoba, 1960; 25/4554)

Alencar, José Martiniano de.
     Credito, O. In per. RTB, num. 293, s/o '56.
     Demônio familiar, O.   (São Paulo : Livraria editora
          Record, 1938; also Rio : Ministério da Educação e
          Cultura, Serviço de Documentação, 1957; 22/5523)
     Rio de Janeiro, O (Verso e reverso.) (Rio : Garnier,
          1937; also in anthol. 28/2656; also in per.
          RTB, num. 300, n/d '57.

Alfonso, Paco.
     Cañaveral. In coll. 20/4200.
     Reivindicación. (La Habana : Imp. Marina de Guerra
          Constitucional, 1936)
     Yari-yari, Mamá Olúa. In coll. 20/4200.
     Yerba hedionda. (La Habana : Editorial Pagrán, 1959;
          23/5301)

Algarra, María Luisa.
     Años de prueba, Los. In anthol. 21/4210.

*Aliber, Alicia and Aliber, Bernardo.
     Caza de herederos. (Buenos Aires : Tespis, 1958; 23/
          5302)
     Sabotaje en el infierno, o, Ese amor terreno. (Méx-
          ico : Ediar Editores Mexicanas, 1959; 23/5303)

Aliber, Bernardo, jt. auth. see under Aliber, Alicia.

*Almeida, Abílio Pereira de.
     Em Moeda Corrente do País. In per. RTB, num.
          324, n/d '61.
     Moral em concordata. In per. RTB, num. 296,
          m/a '57.
     Paiol velho. In per. RTB, num. 273, m/j '53.
     Rua São Luz, 27-8°. In per. RTB, num. 306, n/d
          '58.
     Santa Marta Fabril S. A. (São Paulo : Martins, 1955;
          22/5524)

Alsina, José Arturo.
     Marca de fuego, La. (Asunción, 1926); also in
          anthol. 20/4201.

Alvarez Lleras, Antonio.
     Almas de ahora. (Bogotá : Ed. Centro-instituto gráf.,
          1945; 11/3326)
     Angel de Navidad, El. In coll. 0/16.
     Como los muertos. (Bogotá : Imprenta J. Casis, 1922)

Doctor Bacanotos, El. (Bogotá : Escuelas gráficas
    Salesianas, 1938)
Fuego extraño, El. In coll. 0/16 and 0/17
Mercenarios, Los (Bogotá : Editorial Manique, 1924;
    2nd ed. Escuelas gráficas Salesianas, 1941)
Toma de Granada, La. (Bogotá : Escuelas gráficas
    Salesianas, 194?)
Víboras sociales. In coll. 0/16 and 0/17.
Virrey Solís, El. (Bogotá : Editorial Minerva, 1947)
Zarpazo, El. (Bogotá : Escuelas gráficas Salesianas,
    1938; 12/2746)

Alvarez Ríos, María.
    Víctima, La. (La Habana : Editorial Pagrán, 1959;
        23/5304)

Alvim, Renato and Abreu, Nelson de.
    Amigo Terremoto, O. (Rio : Sociedade Brasileira de
        Autores Teatrais, 1931); also in per. RTB, num.
        262, j/a '51.

Amado, Genolino.
    Avatar. In per. RTB, num. 246, j/a/s '48.

*Amado, Jão Jorge.
    Amor de Castro Alves, O (also known under title Amor
        do soldado.) (Rio : Edições do Polvo, 1947; 2nd
        ed. São Paulo : Martins, 1958; 23/5545)

Amador, Graciela.
    Periquillo y el usurero. In anthol. 0/33.
    Rama y el buey, La. In anthol. 0/33.

Amorim, Enrique.
    Pausa en la selva. In coll. 16/2781.
    Segunda sangre, La. In coll. 16/2781.
    Yo voy más lejos. In coll. 16/2781.

Anaya-Sarmiento, Héctor.
    Adivinaza, La. In per UV/PH, 18, abril/junio 1961,
        p. 313-333 (26/1829)

*Anchieta, José de.
    Auto representado na festa de São Lourenço. (São
        Paulo : Museu Paulista, 1948)
    Vila de Vitória, Na. In coll. 16/2916.
    Visitação de Santa Isabel, Na. In coll. 16/2916.

Ancira, Carlos.
    Después nada. In anthol. 21/4210; also in per.
        PANOR TEAT MEX, 1:5, dic. '54, p. 19-46 (20/
        4202)

*Andrade, Jorge.
    Moratória, A. In anthol. 28/2654; also in per.   TEAT
        BR, 9, a/s '56, p. 13-35 (20/4419)
    Pedreira das Almas. In coll. 24/5796.
    Telescópio, O. In coll. 24/5796.

Angulo y Guridi, Javier.
    Iguaniona. (2nd ed. --Ciudad Trujillo : Montalvo, 1953;
        19/5150)

Aquino, Pedro Benjamín.
    Ha pasado una mujer. (Buenos Aires : Editorial Argen-
        tores, 1935)
    Mujer desconocida, Una. (Buenos Aires : Inst. nacional
        de estudios de teatro, 1945; 11/3327)

*Arango, Gonzalo.
    HK-111. In coll. 24/5600.
    Nada bajo el cielo-raso. In coll. 24/5600.

*Araújo, Nelson Correia de.
    Companhia das Indias, A. (Salvador, Brazil : Pro-
        gresso, 1959; 23/5546)

*Arauz, Alvaro.
    Reina sin sueño, La. In anthol. 24/5643.

*Argüelles, Hugo.
    Camino en la caja. In per.   ES, 3:9, primavera 1958,
        p. 89-96 (22/5300)
    Casa paterna, La. In per.   INBA/R, 2-3, abril-sept.
        '61, p. 33-94 (25/4555)
    Cuervos están de luto, Los. In coll. 26/1830.
    Prodigiosos, Los. (México : Edición Estaciones, 1957;
        21/4201); also in coll. 26/1830.
    Tejedor de milagros, El. In coll. 26/1830.

*Arreola, Juan José.
    Hora de todos, La. (México : Los Presentes, 1954;
        20/4203); also in anthol. 21/4210.

Arriola Ledesma, Abelardo.
    Corazón de India. (Callao : Imp. Perlita, 1935; 1/2114)

Veneno de los hijos, El.   (Callao : Editorial Vida
porteña, 1938)

*Arriví , Francisco.
Club de solteros.   (San Juan : Tinglado Puertorriqueño,
1962; 26/1831); also in coll. 19/5151.
Cóctel de Don Nadie.   In anthol. 28/2292.
María Soledad (also known as Una sombra menos.)
(San Juan : Tinglado Puertorriqueño, 1962; 26/1832);
also in coll. 19/5151.
Medusas en la bahía.   In coll. 24/5601; also in per.
UPRAG/A, año 10, 11:2, abril-junio '55, p. 88-105
(20/4204)
Murciélago, El.   In coll. 24/5601; also in per.
UPRAG/A, año 11, 12:1, enero-marzo '56, p. 71-
85 (20/4205)
Sirena.   (San Juan : Tinglado Puertorriqueño, 1960;
24/5602)
Una sombra menos, see under new title María Soledad.
Vejigantes.   In anthol. 23/5344; also in per. UPRAG/A,
13:1, enero-marzo '57, p. 8-42 (21/4202)

*Arrufat, Antón.
Carnival Saturday.   In PAU/AM, English edition, v. 10,
num. 10, Oct. '58.
Caso se investiga, El.   In coll. 26/1833.
Repetición. La.   In coll. 26/1833.
Ultimo tren, El.   In coll. 26/1833.
Vivo al pollo, El.   In coll. 26/1833; also in anthol.
26/1881.
Zona cero, La.   In coll. 26/1833.

*Asturias, Miguel Angel.
Rayito de estrella.   (Paris, 1929)
Soluna.   (Buenos Aires : Losange, 1955; 21/4203)

Asúnsolo, Enrique.
Antistenes, o, El hijo prodigio.   (México : Editora
Nacional, 1945)
Dos mujeres y una actriz.   In per. HIJO PRODIGO,
ano 3, v. 9, num. 30, sept. '45 and num. 31, oct.
'45 (11/3328)

*Avilés Blonda, Máximo.
Manos vacías, Los.   (Ciudad Trujillo : Arquero, 1959)

Ayala Michelena, Leopoldo.
Al dejar las muñecas.   In coll. 0/19 and 16/2782.

Almas descarnadas. In coll. 16/2782.
Alquilada, La. In coll. 16/2782.
Amor por amor. In coll. 0/19 and 16/2782.
Bagazo. In coll. 0/19 and 16/2782.
Barba no mas, La. In coll. 16/2782.
Dánosle hoy. In coll. 0/18 and 16/2782.
Eco. In coll. 0/18 and 16/2782.
Emoción. (Caracas : Tip. universal, 1925); also in
    coll. 0/18 and 16/2782.
Perra, La. In coll. 16/2782.
Portal de Leoncio Martínez. In coll. 0/19.
Respuesta del otro mundo, La. (Caracas : Editorial
    Elite, 1938); also in coll. 16/2782.
Taquilla, La. In coll. 16/2782.

*Azar, Héctor.
Appasionata, La. (México : El Unicornio, 1958; 23/
    5305); also in anthol. 23/5348.
Olímpica. (México : Fondo de Cultura Económica,
    1962; 26/1834)

Azevedo, Aluizio, jt. auth. see under Azevedo, Arthur.

*Azevedo, Arthur.
Amor por Anexins. In per. RTB, num. 316, j/a '60.
Badejo, O. In per. RTB, num. 288, n/d '55.
Capital federal, A. In per. RTB, num. 298, j/a '57
    (23/5547)
Consulta, Uma. In per. RTB, num. 288, n/d '55.
Cordão, O. In per. RTB, num. 305, s/o '58.
Dote, O. In per. RTB, num. 287, s/o '55.
Fonte Castalia, A. In per. RTB, num. 284, m/a '55.
Oráculo, O. In anthol. 28/2656; also in per. RTB,
    num. 234, abr. '47, and num. 287, s/o '55.
Pele do Lôbo, A. In per. RTB, num. 289, j/f '56.
Retrato a óleo, O. In per. RTB, num. 283, j/f '55.
Véspera de Reis, Uma. In per. TEAT BR, 2, dez '55.
    p. 11-19 (20/4420)
Vida e morte. (Rio : Sociedade Brasileira de Autores
    Teatrais, 1932)

Azevedo, Arthur and Azevedo, Aluizio.
Casa de Orates. In per. RTB, num. 289, j/f '56

Azevedo, Arthur and Piza, José.
Mambembe, O. In per. RTB, num. 290, m/a '56 and
    num. 317, s/o '60.

Azevedo, Arthur and Sampaio, Moreira.
    Genro de muitas sogras, O. In per. RTB, num. 291,
       m/j '56.

Azuela, Mariano.
    Buho en la noche, El. In coll. 4/3980.
    Del Llano Hermanos S. en C. In coll. 4/3980.
    Los de abajo. In coll. 4/3980.

*Badía, Nora.
    Mañana es una palabra. In per. NUEVA GEN, año 1,
       num. 2, feb. '50, p. 5-9 (16/2783)

*Báez, Edmundo.
    Alfiler en los ojos, Un. In anthol. 20/4234.

*Balla, Andrés.
    Estrella y barro (Buenos Aires : Tespis, '59; 24/5603)
    Trapo de piso, El. In anthol. 24/5612.

Baralt, Luis Alejandro.
    Luna en el pantano, La. (La Habana : García, 1936)
    Luna en el río, La. In anthol. 26/1852.
    Tragedia indiana. In anthol. 0/102.

Barbieri, Vicente.
    Facundo en la ciudadela. (Buenos Aires : Losange,
       1956; 23/5306)

Barreiro, José.
    Cheverones, Los. In anthol. 26/1880.

*Barreto, Paulo.
    Ultima noite. In per. RTB, num. 321, m/j '61.

*Barros Grez, Daniel.
    Casi casamiento, El; o, Mientras más vieja más verde.
       In coll. 23/5307.
    Vividor, El. In coll. 23/5307.

*Basurto, Luis G.
    Cada quien su vida. In anthol. 20/4234 and 24/5638.
    Escándalo de la verdad, El. (México : Colección Publi
       teatro, 1960)
    Frente a la muerte. (México : Unión Nacional de
       Autores, 1952; 18/2680)
    Miércoles de ceniza. (México : Costa-Amic, 1956; 21/
       4204)

Reyes del mundo, Los. (México : Col. Teatro Mexicano, 1959; 24/5604); also in anthol. 26/1882.
Toda una dama. In per. PANOR TEAT MÉX, 1:7,
   feb. '55, p. 19-57.

Bayou Herrera, Luis.
   Santos Vega. In anthol. 0/89.

Beccaglia, Juan María.
   Y te harán un santuario. (Buenos Aires : Ministerio de
      Educación y Justicia, 1960; 25/4556)

*Belaval, Emilio S.
   Cielo caído. In anthol. 25/4582.
   Cuando las flores de Pascua son flores de azahar. In
      coll. 0/103.
   Hacienda de los cuatro vientos, La. In anthol. 23/5344.
   Muerte, La. (San Juan : Biblioteca de Autores Puerto-
      rriqueños, 1953; 20/4207)
   Presa de los vencedores, La. In coll. 0/103.
   Vida, La. (Barcelona : Ediciones Rumbos, 1959)

Bellán, José Pedro.
   Blancanieve. (Montevideo, 1929)
   Centinela muerto, El. (Montevideo : J. Florensa, 1930)
   Dios te salve! (Montevideo : C. García, 1920); also in
      anthol. 24/5640.
   Ronda del hijo, La. (Buenos Aires : Teatro nuevo, 1925)

Bellini, Mario, jt. auth.   see under Doblas, Raúl.

Benedetti, Lúcia.
   Banquete, O. In coll. 18/2815.
   Casaco encantado, O. In per. RTB, num. 260, m/a '51.
   Joãozinho anda p'ra trás. (Rio, 1952)
   Simbita e o dragão. In coll. 18/2815.

*Benedetti, Mario.
   Ida y vuelta. (Buenos Aires : Talía, 1963; 26/1835);
      also in anthol. 28/2388b.

*Béneke, Walter.
   Funeral home. (San Salvador : Ministerio de Cultura,
      1959; 23/5308); also in anthol. 28/2388b.
   Paraíso de los imprudentes, El. (San Salvador : Min-
      isterio de Cultura, 1956; 20/4208)

Bengoa, Juan León.
    Dama de las camelias, La. (según A. Dumas hijo.)
        In coll. 0/20.
    Espada desnuda, La.   (Montevideo : Letras, 1950; 16/
        2784)
    Muerta para siempre.   In coll. 0/20.
    Patria en armas, La.   (Montevideo : Letras, 1951; 17/
        2551)
    Sacrificadas, Las.   (Montevideo : Librería Nacional A.
        Barreiro y Ramos, 1922)
    Tu vida y la mía.   (Montevideo, 1935)
    Véstida de ilusión.   In coll. 0/20.

Bengoa, Juan León, jt. auth.   see under Pico, Pedro E.

Bernal, Rafael.
    Antonia.   In coll. 25/4557.
    Maíz en la casa, El.   In coll. 25/4557.
    Paz contigo, La.   In coll. 25/4557.

*Berruti, Alejandro E.
    Historietas de don Alejandro.   In per. TALIA, Supl. 6:
        25, 1964, p. 1-26 (28/2264)
    Les llego su San Martín.   (Buenos Aires : Argentores,
        1934)
    Madre tierra.   (Buenos Aires : Argentores, 1945); also
        in anthol.   24/5626; also in per. ESCENA, año 3,
        num. 127, dic. '20.

Bettencourt, Carlos, jt. auth.   see under Peixoto, Luiz.

*Betti, Atilio.
    Farsa del corazón.   (Buenos Aires : Edición del Teatro
        Estudio, 1953)
    Fundación del desengaño.   (Buenos Aires : Talía, 1960;
        25/4558)

*Bioy Casares, Adolfo, jt. auth.   see under Borges, Jorge
Luis.

Blanco-Amor, Eduardo.
    Amor y crímenes de Juan el Pantera.   In coll. 19/
        5152.
    Angélica en el umbral del cielo.   In coll. 19/5152.
    Verdad vestida, La.   In coll. 19/5152.

Blest Gana, Alberto.
    Jefe de la familia, El.   (Santiago : Zig-Zag, 1956;
        21/4205)

*Bloch, Pedro.
Brasileiros em Nova Iorque. In per. RTB, num. 325,
j/f '62.
Cravo na lapela, Um. In per. RTB, num. 272, m/a
'53.
Dona Xepa. In per. RTB, num. 303, m/j '58.
Flauta para o negro, Uma. In per. RTB, num. 314,
m/a '60.
Inimigos não mandam flores, Os. In coll. 22/5525.
Irene. (Rio : Editora talmagráfica, 1953)
Leonora (transl. into Spanish.) (Montevideo : Ediciones
Mensaje, 1953)
Mãos de Eurídice, As. In coll. 22/5525; also in anthol.
28/2654.
Miquelina. In per. RTB, num. 318, n/d '60.
Problema, O. In coll. 0/21.
Sorriso de pedra, O. In coll. 0/21.

Blonda, Máximo Avilés see Avilés Blonda, Máximo.

*Bocanegra, Matías de.
Sufrir para merecer. In per. MAGN/B, 20, num. 3,
julio-sept. 1949, p. 379-459 (15/2179)

Bocayuva, Quintino.
Família, A. In per. RTB, num. 294, n/d '56.

Bofanini, Darcília Azarany.
Retalhos da vida. In coll. 12/2938.
Unico beijo. In coll. 12/2938.

Bollo, Sarah.
Pola Salavarrieta. (Montevideo : Ed. Claudio García,
1945; 12/2747)

*Borba Filho, Hermilo.
Barca de ouro, A. In coll. 21/4326.
Electra no circo. In coll. 21/4326.
João sem terra. In coll. 21/4326.

Borba Filho, Hermilo, jt. auth. see under Oliveira, Valdemar de.

Borba, Hermilo. see Borba Filho, Hermilo

Borges, Jorge Luis and Bioy Casares, Adolfo.
Orilleros, Los. In coll. 21/4206.
Paraíso de los creyentes, El. In coll. 21/4206.

*Borges, José Carlos Cavalcânti.
  Acima do bem-querer.   (Rio : Editôra Letras e artes,
    1964; 28/2649)

Borrás, Eduardo.
  Amorina.   (Buenos Aires : Tespis, 1957; 22/5301)
  Proceso Ferrer, El.   (Barcelona : Mancci, 1932)

Boscoli, Geysa and Santos, Miguel.
  Estação de "Aguias". In per. RTB, num. 240, out. '47.

Bourbakis, Roberto.
  Gorgona, La. In per. R LYCEUM, v. 8, num. 28,
    nov. '51, p. 93-106 (17/2552)

Brau, Salvador.
  Vuelta al hogar, La. In anthol. 26/1883.

Bravo Garzón, Roberto.
  Viento sobre las aguas.   (Xalapa : Univ. Veracruzana,
    1962; 26/1836)

Bressan, Alma.
  Adiós mama Claudia.   (Buenos Aires : Tespis, 1959;
    26/1837)

Brierre, Jean Fernand.
  Adiós a la marsellesa, El. In coll. 19/5380.
  Aïeules, Les.   (Port-au-Prince : Henri Deschamps,
    1950; 16/2935)
  Belle.   (Port-au-Prince : Imprimerie de l'état, 1948)
  Drapeau de demain, Le.   (Port-au-Prince : Imprimerie
    haïtienne, 1931)
  Pétion et Bolívar (Spanish version : Pétion y Bolívar.)
    In coll. 19/5380.

Brook, Paulita.
  Entre cuatro paredes.   (México : Talleres gráficos de
    la nación, 1942)
  Jóvenes, Los.   (Mexico : B. Costa-Amic, 1959; 23/5310)

Bruno, Jorge.
  Cuarto de Anatol, El.   (Montevideo : El Tinglado, 1956;
    20/4209)

Bruno, Pedro Mariano.
  Semana sin domingo.   (Buenos Aires : Tespis, 1962;
    26/1838)

Buch, René A.
 Caracola vacía, La. In per. R LYCEUM, v. 8, num. 26,
  mayo '51, p. 111-136 (17/2553)

*Buenaventura, Enrique.
 En la diestra de Dios Padre. In coll. 26/1839; also in
  anthol. 28/2388b.
 Requiem por el padre Las Casas, Un. In coll. 26/1839.
 Tragedia del Rey Christophe, La. In coll. 26/1839.

Buffo, Guido.
 Lazos invisibles. (Córdoba, Arg. , 1947)

Buitrago, Fanny.
 Distancias doradas, Las. In coll. 28/2265.
 Hombre de paja, El. In coll. 28/2265.

*Bustillo Oro, Juan.
 Justicia, s. a. In coll. 0/26.
 Los que vuelven. In coll. 0/26.
 Masas. In coll. 0/26.
 San Miguel de las Espinas. (México : Sociedad General de
  Autores de México, 1948; 14/2950); also in anthol.
  20/4234

*Buttaro, Enrique.
 Fumadas. In anthol. 21/4209.

Caldera, Daniel.
 Tribunal de honor, El. In per. UCC/FT, 4:13, 1. tri-
  mestre '57, p. 105-127 (22/5302)

Calderón, Fernando.
 A ninguna de las tres. (México : UNAM, 1944)
 Ana Bolena. In coll. 23/5311.
 Hernán o la vuelta del cruzado. (México : Secretaria de
  Educación pública, 1945); also in coll. 23/5311.
 Muerte de Virginia por la libertad de Roma. (México :
  UNAM, 1960; 24/5605)
 Torneo, El. In coll. 23/5311.

*Callado, Antônio.
 Cidade assassinada, A. (Rio : J. Olympio, 1954; 19/5352)
 Frankel. (Rio : Ministério da Educação e Cultura, Serviço
  da Documentação, 1955); also in TEAT BR, 7, m/j '56,
  p. 15-33 (20/4421)
 Pedro Mico. In per. RTB, num. 326, m/a '62.

Tesouro de Chica da Silva, O. In per RTB, num. 326,
    m/a '62.

Calvente de Helmbold, Ana María.
    Mariano Moreno. (Rosario, Arg. : Lib. y ed. Ruiz,
        1939; 7/3772)

Calvillo Madrigal, Salvador.
    Amanecer. In HIJO PRODIGO, año 3, v. 10.   num. 33
        dic. '45, p. 171-178 (11/3329)

Camargo, Christovão de.
    Principe galante, O. (Rio : Ed. A Noite, 1921; 7/4989a)

*Camargo, Joracy.
    Amigo da família, O. (Rio : Sociedade Brasileira de
        Autores Teatrais, 1951; 17/2645)
    Anastácio. (São Paulo : Edições Cultura Brasileira,
        1937; also Rio : Z. Valverde 1945; 11/3440)
    Bôbo do rei, O. (Rio : Sociedade Brasileira de Autores
        Teatrais, 1932; also Editora Minerva, 1937); also in
        per. RTB, num. 280, j/a '54.
    Burro, O. (Rio : Z. Valverde, 1945; 11/3441)
    Chauffeur. (Rio : Sociedade Brasileira de Autores
        Teatrais, 1937)
    Corpo de luz, Um. In coll. 0/23.
    Deus lhe pague. (Rio : Minerva, 193?; also Valverde,
        1945; also Simões, 1953; also in Spanish as Dios se
        lo pague, Buenos Aires : Argentores, 1935; also
        Madrid, 1951); also in coll. 0/23 and 0/25.; also
        in per. RTB, num. 302, m/a '58.
    Figueira do inferno. In coll. 0/23.
    Grande remedio. In coll. 0/25.
    Mania de grandesa. (Rio : Edição Talmagráfica da
        Papeleria Coelho, 1944)
    Maria Cachucha. (Rio : Valverde, 1940)
    Neto de Deus, O. (Rio : Valverde, 1945)
    Pupila dos meus olhos, A. (Rio : Valverde, 1945;
        11/3442)
    Sábio, O. (Rio : Valverde, 1945)
    Santa Madre, A. (Rio : Simões, 1954)

Cambours Ocampo, Arturo.
    Delirio del viento, El. (Buenos Aires : Librería Per-
        lado, 1948; 14/2951)
    Max, la maravilla del mundo. (Buenos Aires : Tor, '35)
    Mujer vestida de silencio, Una. (Buenos Aires :
        Occidente, 1940)

Campos, Eduardo.
    Demónio e a rosa, O. In per. CLA, año 1, num. 1,
        fev. '48, p. 5-27 (14/3074)

*Campos, Geir.
    Sonho de Calabar, O. (Rio : Livraria São José, 1959;
        23/5548)

Campos, Maria Jacinta Trovão de see Trovão de Campos,
    Maria Jacinta

Canal-Feijóo, Bernardo.
    Casos de Juan, Los. (Buenos Aires : Talía, 1961;
        26/1840)

*Cañas, Alberto.
    Luto robado, El. (San José : Editorial Costa Rica,
        1963; 26/1841)

*Cantón, Wilberto.
    Escuela de cortesanos. (México : Helio-México, 1956;
        20/4210)
    Inolvidable. (México : Ecuador, 1961; 25/4559)
    Jardín de las gorgonas, El. In anthol. 24/5644.
    Malditos. (México : Colección Teatro Mexicano, 1959;
        23/5312); also in anthol. 23/5343.
    Nocturno a Rosario, El. (México : Los Presentes,
        1956; 21/4207)
    Nosotros somos Dios. In per. UV/PH, 2. época, 26,
        abril/junio '63, p. 315-376 (28/2266)
    Nota roja. (México : Ecuador, 1965; 28/2267)
    Saber morir. In per. CAM, v. 51, num. 3, m/j '50,
        p. 233-288 (16/2785)

Capablanca, Enrique G. de.
    Botija y la felicidad, La. In anthol. 25/4571.

Capdevila, Arturo.
    Amor de Schahrazada, El. In coll. 0/24.
    Arabes, Los. In coll. 0/24.
    Casa de los fantasmas, La. (Buenos Aires : Gleizer,
        1926)
    Joán Garín e Satanás. (Barcelona : Instituto Gráfico
        Oliva de Vilanova, 1935; 1/2110)
    Sulamita, La. (Buenos Aires : Losada?, 1920)

Caraco, Alberto.
    Inès de Castro (in French). In coll. 7/4990.

Martyrs de Cordou, Les. (in French.) In coll. 7/4990.

*Carballido, Emilio.
    Amor muerto, El. In coll. 21/4208.
    Bodega, La. In coll. 21/4208.
    Censo, El. In coll. 26/1842.
    Cuento de navidad, Un. In coll. 26/1842.
    Danza que sueña la tortuga, La. In anthol. 20/4234.
    Día que se soltaron los leones, El. In coll. 23/5313.
    Escribir, por ejemplo. In coll. 26/1842.
    Espejo, El. In coll. 26/1842.
    Estatuas de marfil, Las. (Xalapa : Universidad Vera-
        cruzana, 1960; 24/5606)
    Felicidad. In anthol. 21/4210.
    Glaciar, El. In coll. 21/4208.
    Hebra de oro, La. In coll. 21/4208.
    Lugar y la hora, El. (México : Revista America, 1951)
    Medalla, La. In coll. 26/1842.
    Medalla al mérito. (México : Revista America, 1949)
    Medusa. In coll. 23/5313.
    Misa primera. In 26/1842.
    Parásitas. In coll. 26/1842.
    Paso de madrugada. In coll. 26/1842.
    Pequeño día de ira, Un. (La Habana : Casa de las
        Américas, 1962)
    Perfecta casada, La. In coll. 26/1842; also in per.
        UV/PH, 20, oct-dic '61, p. 685-691 (26/1843)
    Relojero de Córdoba, El. In coll. 23/5313.
    Rosalba y los llaveres. In coll. 23/5313; also in per.
        PANOR TEAT MEX, 1:9, m/j '55, p. 21-67
        (20/4211)
    Selaginela. In coll. 26/1842.
    Silencio, pollos pelones, ya les van a echar su maíz!
        In anthol. 28/2306; also in per. UV/PH, 2. época,
        31, julio/sept. '64. p. 509-571 (28/2268)
    Solitario en octubre, El. In coll. 26/1842.
    Tangentes. In coll. 26/1842; also in anthol. 24/5643.
    Teseo. In per. UV/PH, 24, oct-dic. '62, p. 651-673
        (26/1844)
    Zona intermedia, La. (México : Unión Nacional de
        Autores, 1950)

Carballido, Emilio and Hernández, Luisa Josefina.
    Pastores de la ciudad. In coll. 26/1842; also in per.
        UV/PH, 12, oct./dic. '59 (23/5314)

Carballido, Emilio and Magaña, Sergio.
    Suplicante, El. In per. UNAM/UM, 13:4, dic. '58,
        p. 8-11 (22/5303)

Carballo de Núñez, Carlota.
    Tacita de plata, La. In anthol. 12/2766.

*Cardoso, Lúcio.
    Escravo, O. (Rio : Valverde, 1945; 11/3443)
    Filho pródigo, O. In per. COLEGIO, año 2, num. 5,
        p. 41-86 (15/2555)

*Cardozo, Joaquim.
    Coronel de Macambira, O. (Rio : Editôra Civilização
        Brasileira, 1963; 28/2650)

Cariola Villagrán, Carlos.
    Entre gallos y medianoche. (Santiago : Librería Hem-
        ette y Frías, 1920); also in per. UCC/FT, 4:13,
        1. trimestre '57, p. 35-61 (22/5304)
    On parle français (se habla castellano). (Santiago :
        Nascimento, 1923)

*Carlino, Carlos.
    Biunda, La. (Buenos Aires : Editorial Ambar, 1955);
        also in coll. 20/4212.
    Cabello sobre la almohada, Un. In coll. 24/5607.
    Cuando trabaje. In coll. 24/5607.
    Esa vieja serpiente engañadora. In coll. 24/5607.
    Tierra del destino. In coll. 20/4212.

Carneiro, Nelson.
    Culpado foi você, O. In per. RTB, num. 266, m/a
        '52.

Carvalho, Afonso de.
    Chalaça, O. In per. RTB, num. 274, j/a '53.

Carvalho, Fernando Livino de.
    Há sempre um amanhã. (Recife : Gráfica Editôra do
        Recife, 1959; 23/5549)

Casas, Myrna.
    Cristal roto en el tiempo. In anthol. 25/4582.

Castillero Reyes, Ernesto de Jesús.
    Montezumas, Los. In per. UNIV PAN, num. 26,
        primer semestre '48, p. 45-68 (13/2224)

*Castillo, Abelardo.
　　Israfel. (Buenos Aires : Losada, 1964; 28/2270)
　　Otro Judas, El; o, El pájaro mágico. (Buenos Aires,
　　　　1961; 25/4560)

Castillo de González, Aurelio.
　　Voluntad de Dios, La. In per. CUBN/R, 2. serie, 8:2,
　　　　abril-junio '57, p. 7-35 (22/5305)

Castillo F. , Ricardo.
　　Voz en el viento, Una. In per. REV INDIAS, num. 98,
　　　　j/a '51 (13/2225)

Castorena, José de Jesús.
　　De Campanario o Democalotlan. In per. AMERICA,
　　　　época nueva, num. 60, 1949, p. 225-303 (15/
　　　　2435)

Castro Saavedra, Carlos.
　　Historia de un jaulero. (Medellín : Aguirre Editor,
　　　　1960; 26/1845)

Catani, Enrique.
　　Bosque, El. (La Plata : Ediciones Revista, 1948)
　　Tren pasa al oeste, Un. (La Plata : Municipalidad de
　　　　La Plata, 1962; 26/1846)

Catania, Carlos.
　　Nube en la alcantarilla, La. In per. TALIA, supl. ,
　　　　3:21, '61, p. 1-22 (28/2271)

Cayol, Roberto L.
　　Debut de la Piba, El. In anthol. 21/4209.

Cecco, Sergio Amadeo de.
　　Reñidero, El. (Buenos Aires : Talía, 1963; 28/2272)

Centurión Miranda, R. , jt. auth. see under Plá, Josefina.

Cepelos, Batista.
　　Maria Madalena. In per. RTB, num. 304, j/a '58.

Certad, Aquiles.
　　Cuando quedamos trece. (Caracas : Impresores Unidos,
　　　　1943)
　　Cuando Venus tuvo brazos. In coll. 17/2554.
　　Hombre que no tuvo tiempo de morir, El. In coll.
　　　　17/2554.

Julieta engaña a Romeo. (Carcacas, 1952)
Lo que faltaba a Eva. (Caracas : Editorial Elite, 1943)
Serpiente sobre la alfombra, La. In coll. 17/2554.

Cervantes, Dagoberto de.
Adiós, Mamá Carlota. (México : Los Presentes, 1955)
Lorenzo, corrido del vengador. (México : Helio-Mexico,
1954; 19/5153)
Orestes, el hombre. (México : Editorial Mascaras,
1946)

*Césaire, Aimé.
Et les chiens se taisaient. (Paris : Présence Africaine,
1956)
Tragédie du roi Christophe, La. (Paris : Présence
Africaine, 1963; 26/2123)

Chacón.
Hombre de la gallina, El. In anthol. 26/1880.

*Chalbaud, Román.
Sagrado y obsceno. (Caracas : Tipografía Iberia, 1961;
28/2273)

Chesta Aránguiz, José.
Umbral, El. (Santiago : Ediciones Alerce, 1962;   26/
1847)

Chioino, José.
Propia comedia, La. (Lima : Círculo Peruano de Autor-
es, 1949; 15/2436)
Provinciano, El, o La divina canción. (Lima, 1935)

*Chocrón, Isaac.
Quinto infierno, El. (Caracas : Ediciones Zodíaco,
1961; 26/1848)

*Cid Pérez, José.
Hombres de dos mundos. In anthol. 0/102.

Coelho Netto, Henrique Maximiano see Neto, Coelho.

Coelho Netto, Paulo.
Imortal, O. (Rio : Editôra Melso, 1962; 28/2651)
Metamorfose. (Rio : Simões, 1959)

Cogolani, Roberto Dante.
Desván para el ensueño, Un. In coll. 25/4561.

Mañana. In coll. 25/4561.
Nada más. In coll. 25/4561.
Otro, El. In coll. 25/4561.

Conrado, Aldomar.
Livro de David, O. (Recife : Secretaria da Educação
e Cultura de Pernambuco, 1958; 23/5550)

Córdoba Romero, Guillermo.
José Antonio Galán. (Bucaramanga, 1947); also in per.
REV AMERICA, v. 11, num. 36, dic. '50, p. 385-
431 (13/2226)

Cordone, Rogelio, jt. auth. see under Goicochea, Carlos.

Córdova, Luis.
Tijeras y listones. (México : Los Presentes, 1956;
21/4211)

*Coronel Urtecho, José, jt. auth. see under Pasos, Joaquin.

Correa, Julio.
Ñane mba' era' ĩn (in Guaraní and Spanish) (Asunción :
Editorial Ortíz Guerrero, 1965; 28/2274)

Correa, Pancho.
Cántios rebeldes. In coll. 13/2227.
Derecho a los hijos, El. In coll. 13/2227.
Doña Zolla. In coll. 13/2227.
Flor de Muguet. In coll. 13/2227.
Jardín del amor, El. In coll. 13/2227.
Maquí , El. In coll. 13/2227.
Ocaso de un rey, El. In coll. 13/2227.
Sacrificio, El. In coll. 13/2227.

*Corrêa, Viriato.
Linguiceiros Roderiz, Os. In per. RTB, num. 275,
s/o '53.
Moela da Galinda, A. In per. RTB, num. 275, s/o
'53.
Pobre diabo. In per. RTB, num. 245, m/j '48.
Sombra dos laranjais, A. In per. REV ACAD BRAS
LET, v. 73, jan-junho '46, p. 127-216 (13/2344)
Tiradentes. (Rio : Gráfica Guarany, 1941; 8/4317)

Correia, Manuel Viriato see Corrêa, Viriato.

Cortinas, Ismael.
    Credo, El. In coll. 7/4708.
    Farsa cruel. In coll. 7/4708.
    Rosa natural, La. In coll. 7/4708.

*Cossa, Roberto M.
    Nuestro fin de semana. (Buenos Aires : Talía, 1964;
        28/2275; also N. Y. : Macmillan, 1966; 28/2276)

Costantini, Humberto.
    Estimado prócer. In coll. 28/2277.
    Llave, La. In coll. 28/2277.
    Señor alto, rubio, de bigotes, Un. In coll. 28/2277.

Crimi, Humberto.
    Actor, El. In coll. 23/5315.
    Otra versión, La. In coll. 23/5315.

Cruz, Eddy Dias da see Rebêlo, Marques.

*Cruz, Sor Juana Inés de la.
    Sainete segundo. In anthol. 22/5315.

*Cuadra, Pablo Antonio.
    Por los caminos van los campesinos. In anthol. 23/
        5346; also in anthol. 28/2388b.

Cunha, Humberto.
    Vida tem três andares, Al. (Rio : Sociedade Brasileira
        de Autores Teatrais, 1951; 17/2646)

*Cuzzani, Agustín.
    Centro-forward murió al amanecer, El. (Buenos Aires :
        Ariadna, 1955; 19/5154); also in coll. 24/5608.
    Indios estaban cabreros, Los. In coll. 24/5608.
    Sempronio. In coll. 24/5608; also in anthol. 28/2388b.
    Una libra de carne. (Buenos Aires : Quetzal, 1954;
        21/4212): also in coll. 24/5608.

Dantas, Raymundo Souza.
    Desespero de Job. In per. PROV SAO PEDRO, num.
        13, marĉo-junho '51, p. 40-48 (15/2556)

Dauphin, Marcel.
    Boisrond-Tonnerre (Port-au-Prince : Dorsinville, 1954;
        19/5384)
    Pierre Sully. (Port-au-Prince, Imprimerie de l'Etat,
        1960; 26/2126)

Dávalos, Juan Carlos.
 Aguila renga. (Buenos Aires : Roldán, 1928)
 Tierra en armas, La. (Buenos Aires : Condor, 1935;
  1/2111)

Dávalos, Marcelino.
 Así pasan. (México : UNAM, 1945; also in anthol.
  20/4234.)

Daycard, Enriqueta.
 Caballo rojo bajo el sofá, El. In per UCCH/A, 15,
  sep. '61, p. 34-43 (28/2278)

*Debesa, Fernando.
 Mama Rosa. (Santiago : Editorial del Nuevo Extremo,
  1958; 22/5306)

*Defilippis Novoa, Francisco.
 Caminos del Mundo, Los. (Buenos Aires : Editorial
  Claridad, 1936)
 He visto a Dios. In anthol. 24/5627.

*Denevi, Marco.
 Emperado de la China, El. (Buenos Aires : Ediciones
  Aguaviva, 1060; 25/4562)
 Expedientes, Los. (Buenos Aires : Talía, 1957; 21/
  4213)

D'Erzell, Catalina.
 Pecado de las mujeres, El. (México : Sociedad General
  de Autores de México, 1947; 14/2953)

De Stefani, Alejandro, jt. auth.   see under Tálice, Roberto
 Alejandro.

Deugenio, Rubén.
 Ascenso, El. In coll. 26/1849.
 Quiniela. In coll. 26/1849.

*Díaz Díaz, Oswaldo.
 Blondinette. (Bogotá : Editorial ABC, 1942); also in
  coll. 28/2280.
 Boda de Caperucita. In coll. 28/2280.
 Cada mayo una rosa. In coll. 28/2280.
 Claver. In coll. 28/2280.
 Comedia famosa de doña Antonia Quijana. (Bogotá :
  Universidad Nacional de Colombia, 1950); also in

per. REV INDIAS, num. 100, oct. -dic. '51 (13/
2228)

Desdémona ha muerto. In coll. 28/2280.

Dos estampas del 20 de julio. In coll. 28/2280.

En vela. In coll. 28/2280.

Expreso. In coll. 28/2280.

Gaitana, La. (Bogota, 1941)

Galán. In coll. 28/2280; also in per. REV AMERICA,
v. 2, num. 6, junio '46, p. 312-317 (11/3330);
also in per. REV INDIAS, num. 96, mayo '50,
p. 479-507 (13/2229)

Hora azul 3 a. m. In coll. 28/2280.

Reina Juana. In coll. 28/2280.

Señal de Caín. In coll. 28/2280.

Sueño de una noche de septiembre. In coll. 28/2280.

Y los sueños, sueños son. (Bogotá: Espiral, 1951;
17/2556); also in coll. 28/2280.

Díaz Dufóo, Carlos.
Padre Mercader. (México : Imprenta Manuel Lerin
Sánchez, 1929); also in anthol. 20/4234.

*Díaz González, Olallo.
Detallistas, Los. In anthol. 26/1880.
Efectos de billete, Los, o A la celaduría. In anthol.
26/1880.

*Díaz, Jorge.
Variaciones para muertos en percusión. In per. CDLA/
CO, 1, julio-agosto '64, p. 17-48 (28/2279)

Díaz Sánchez, Ramón.
Debajo de estos aleros. In per. TEATRO, 16, mayo-
agosto '55, p. 55-77 (20/4213)

Díez Barroso, Victor Manuel.
Buena suerte. In coll. 0/22.
El y su cuerpo. (México : Mundial, 1934)
En "El Riego". In coll. 0/22.
Estampas. (México, 1932)
Farsa, Una. (México : Nación, 1928)
Muñeca rota, La. In coll. 0/22.
Nocturno. In coll. 0/22.
Qué le hace que no sea cierto! In coll. 0/22.
Véncete a ti mismo. (México : Nación, 1926); also in
anthol. 20/4234.
Verdad y mentira. In coll. 0/22.

*Discépolo, Armando.
      Babilonia. In anthol. 21/4209.
      Mateo. In coll. 24/5609.
      Relojero. (Buenos Aires : Argentores, 1934); also in
          coll. 24/5609.
      Stéfano. In coll. 24/5609.

Discépolo, Armando and Discépolo, Enrique Santos.
      Organito, El. In anthol. 24/5627.

*Discépolo, Enrique Santos.
      Blum. (Buenos Aires : Sociedad General de Autores de
          la Argentina, 1952)

Discépolo, Enrique, jt. auth. see under Discépolo, Armando.

Doblas, Raúl and Bellini, Mario.
      Rebellión de los fenómenos, La. (Buenos Aires : Tespis,
          1963; 28/2281)

*Domingos, Anselmo.
      Cem gramas de homem. In per. RTB, num. 241,
          n '47.

Domínguez, Franklin.
      Amigo desconocido nos aguarda, Un. (Ciudad Trujillo,
          1958; 23/5316)
      Broma del senador, La. In 23/5317.
      Niña que quería ser princesa, La. In anthol. 23/5318.
      Ultimo instante, El. In coll. 23/5318.

Domínguez, Pablo.
      Tremedal. (Caracas : Asociacón de Escritores Vene-
          zolanos, 1952; 18/2682)

Dow, Alberto.
      Diablo, el Angel y la mujer, El. In coll. 17/2557.
      Sangre petrificada, La. In coll. 17/2557.

Dracco-Bracco, Adolfo.
      Se han deshojado en el jardín las rosas. (Quetzal-
          tenango : Centro editorial, 1938; 4/3981)

Dragún, Osvaldo.
      Historia de mi esquina. In coll. 28/2284.
      Historias para ser contadas. (Buenos Aires : Talía,
          21/4214); also in coll. 28/2283; also in per. PRIA,
          35, jun/jul '62, p. 14-33 (28/2282)

Jardín del infierno, El. In per. INBA/R, 5, '62,
  p. 51-81 (28/2283)
Los de la mesa 10. In coll. 28/2284.
Milagro en el mercado viejo. In anthol. 28/2285.
Peste viene de Melos, La. (Buenos Aires : Ariadna,
  1956; 20/4214)
Tupac Amarú. (Buenos Aires : Losange, 1957; 21/
  4215)
Y nos dijeron que éramos inmortales. (Xalapa : Univ.
  Veracruzana, 1962; 26/1850)

Ducasse, Vendenesse.
  Fort de Joux: ou, Les derniers moments de Toussaint
    Louverture. (Port-au-Prince : Editions Veteran,
    1964; 28/2690)

*Eichelbaum, Samuel.
  Aguas del mundo, Las. (Buenos Aires : Tespis, 1959)
  Divorcio nupcial. In coll. 0/31; also in anthol. 20/
    4201.
  Dogman, El. (Buenos Aires, 1922)
  Dos brasas. In coll. 18/2683; also in anthol. 23/5309.
  En tu vida estoy yo. (Buenos Aires : Gleizer, 1934)
  Gato y su selva, El. In coll. 18/2683.
  Guapo del 900, Un. (Buenos Aires : Talleres gráficos
    La Argentina, 1940); also in coll. 18/2683; also in
    anthol. 22/5315.
  Hermana terca, La. (Buenos Aires : Claridad, 1924)
  Hogar, Un. (Buenos Aires : Gleizer, 1923)
  Instinto. In coll. 0/34.
  Mala sed, La. (Buenos Aires : Ediciones Selectas
    América, 1920); also in coll. 0/32.
  N. N. Homicida. In anthol. 0/30.
  Pájaro de barro. (Buenos Aires : Sur, 1940); also in
    coll. 18/2683.
  Rostro perdido. In per. IJACI/C, 4:13, oct-dic. '56,
    p. 63-86 (23/5319)
  Ruedo de las almas, El. In per. ESCENA, año 6,
    num. 259, jun '23.
  Señorita. (Buenos Aires : El Inca, 1931)
  Soledad es tu nombre. In coll. 0/32.
  Tal Servando Gómez, Un. (Buenos Aires : Losange,
    1954; 19/5155); also in coll. 0/31.
  Vergüenza de querer. In coll. 0/31.

Eichelbaum, Samuel, jt. auth. see under Pico, Pedro E.

Eiró, Paulo.
    Sangue limpo. In per. AM/R, año 14, v. 118, abril-
       junho '47, p. 21-98 (14/3075)

Elorduy, Aquiles.
    Canción de Tata Nacho y unos versos de Manuel Acuña.
       In coll. 0/29.
    Juguetes, Los. (México, 1931); also in coll. 0/29.
    Mano izquierda, La. In coll. 0/29.
    Mi cuarto a espadas. In coll. 0/29.

Encina, Juan de la see Asunsolo, Enrique.

Epiñeira, Antonio.
    En la puerta del horno. In anthol. 22/5329.

Ercilla, Alonso de.
    Prueba, La (based on La Araucana.) In anthol. 18/2698.

Ernhard, James.
    Comedia para asesinos. In per. UCC/FT, 4:13, 1.
       trimestre '57, p. 63-103 (22/5307)

Espejo, Beatriz.
    Luna en el charco, La. In per. ES, 19, otoño '60,
       p. 79-88 (24/5611)

*Estorino, Abelardo.
    Robo del cichino, El. In anthol. 26/1881 and 28/2388b.

Estrada, Ricardo.
    Ella y él. (Guatemala : Imp. Universitaria, 1956; 20/
       4215)
    Ratón Pérez. (Guatemala : Editorial Popol Vuh, 1955)

Fabiani, Víctor.
    Perros ladran a la luna, Los. In anthol. 24/5612.

Fabregat Cúneo, Roberto.
    Como por arte de magia. In per. UMIP/RN, v. 13,
       num. 139, julio '50 p. 85-120, and num. 140, ag.
       '50, p. 150-272 (16/2786)
    Dama del retrato premiado. In per. UMIP/RN, v. 12,
       num. 121, enero '49, p. 70-82 (15/2437)
    Luces del cine. In coll. 0/27.
    Pinar de Tierras Altas, El. In per. UMIP/RN, v. 15,
       num. 179, nov. '53, p. 181-229 (20/4216)

Verdad llega de noche, La.   In coll. 0/27.

Faria, Octávio de.
    Judas.   In coll. 5/3970.
    Pilatos.   In coll. 5/3970.
    Yokanaan.   In coll. 5/3970.

Faro, Arnaldo, jt. auth.   see under   Sampaio, José Silveira.

Feder, Carlos Eduardo.
    Día y la noche, El.   In coll. 18/2684.
    Dignidad de Beatriz, La.   In coll. 18/2684.
    Esperanza del mar, La.   In coll. 0/1.
    Felipe y Santiago.   In coll. 18/2684.
    Gallina de los huevos de oro, La.   In coll. 0/2.
    Herencia de águeda, La.   In coll. 0/1.
    Juventud del cedro, La.   In coll. 0/2.
    Puntadas de un sastre.   In coll. 0/2.
    Silla mágica, La.   In coll. 0/1.
    Sueño de una mañana de verano.   In coll. 0/3.
    Sueño de una tarde de invierno.   In coll. 0/3.

Feijóo, Samuel.
    Alegre noticia, La.   In anthol. 26/1852.

Fein, María Teresa.
    Húsar, El.   In coll. 18/2685.
    Río viene bajando, El.   In coll. 18/2685.

*Felipe, Carlos.
    Capricho en rojo.   (La Habana : Pagrán, 1959; 23/5320)
    Chinois, El.   In coll. 26/1851.
    Ladrillos de plata.   In coll. 26/1851.
    Requiem por Yarini.   In anthol. 26/1852.
    Travieso Jimmy, El.   In coll. 26/1851; also in anthol.
        0/102.

*Fernandes, Millôr.
    Bruito como um deus.   In coll. 21/4327.
    Do tamanho de um defunto.   In coll. 21/4327.
    Elefante no caos, Um.   (Rio : Editôra do Editor,
        1955)
    Gaivota, A.   In coll. 21/4327.
    Mulher em três atos, Uma.   In coll. 21/4327.

Fernandes, Nabor.
    Inveja em dez capitulos.   (São Paulo : Brescia, 1946;
        12/2939)

*Fernández de Lizardi, José Joaquín.
    Auto Mariano. In coll. 28/2287.
    Negro sensible, El. In coll. 28/2287; also in per.
        INBA/CBA, 1:2, sept. '60, p. 57-75 (28/2286)
    Noche más venturosa, La. (México : Librería Franco
        Americana, 1924)
    Pastorela en dos actos. In coll. 28/2287.
    Periquillo sarmiento, El. (México : UNAM, 1962; 26/
        1853)
    Todos contra el payo y el payo contra todos. In coll.
        28/2287.
    Tragedia del Padre Arenas, La. In coll. 28/2287.
    Unipersonal de Don Agustín de Iturbide. In 28/2287.
    Unipersonal del Arcabuceado. In coll. 28/2287.

Fernández, Piri.
    De tanto caminar. In anthol. 25/4582.

Fernández Suárez, Alvaro.
    Retablo de Maese Pedro, El.   (Montevideo : Ed. Letras,
        1946; 12/2748)

Fernández Unsain, José María.
    Dos basuras. (Buenos Aires : Tespis, 1957; 22/5308)
    Muerte se está poniendo vieja, La. (Buenos Aires :
        Argentores, 1947)

*Ferrari Amores, Alfonso.
    A la sombra del alto manzano. In coll. 28/2288.
    Sábanas blancas, Las. In coll. 28/2288.

*Ferrer, Rolando.
    A las siete, la estrella. In coll. 26/1854.
    Corte, El. In coll. 26/1854.
    El que mató al responsable. In coll. 26/1854.
    Fiquito. In coll. 26/1854.
    Función homenaje. In coll. 26/1854.
    Hija de Nacho, La. In coll. 26/1854.
    Lila la mariposa. In coll. 26/1854.
    Próceres, Los. In coll. 26/1854.
    Taza de café, La. In coll. 26/1854.

*Ferretti, Aurelio.
    Bodas del diablo, Las. (Buenos Aires : Argentores,
        1948)
    Café de Euterpe, El. In coll. 28/2289.
    Cama y el sofá, La. In coll. 28/2289.
    Farsa de farsas. In coll. 18/2686.

Farsa del consorte. In coll. 18/2686.
Farsa del héroe y el villano. In coll. 18/2686.
Farsa del hombre y el queso. In coll. 18/2686.
Fidela. (Buenos Aires : Tespis, 1961; 26/1855); also
    in coll. 18/2686.
Histrión. In coll. 28/2289.
Multitud, La. (Buenos Aires : Tinglado, 1946; 12/
    2749)
Pasión de Justo Pómez, La. In coll. 28/2289.
Pum ... en el ojo! In coll. 28/2289.

*Figueiredo, Guilherme.
    Asilado, O. In per. RTB, num. 328, j/a '62.
    Deus dormiu lá em casa, Um. (In English as God
        slept here. Rio : Ministério da Educação e Cultura,
        Serviço de Documentação, 1957; 24/5798); also in
        French as Un dieu a dormi dans la maison in per
        FRANCE ILLUSTRATION, suppl. théatral, num. 117,
        oct. '52.
    Lady Godiva. In per. RTB, num. 252, j/a/s '49.
    Rapôsa e as uvas, A. (In Spanish as La zorra y las
        uvas. Buenos Aires : Losange, 1955); also in
        anthol. 28/2654.
    Tragédia para rir. (Rio : Civilização brasileira, 1958;
        22/5526)

Flores Chinarro, Francisco.
    Cuidado con las jaranas. (Lima : Taller de Linotipia,
        1950; 16/2787)

*Florit, Eugenio.
    Estella, La. (La Habana : García, 1947; 13/2230)

Folino, Norberto.
    Ave del desierto, El. (Buenos Aires : Librería Perlado,
        1959; 23/5321)

Fonseca, José Paulo M. da.
    Dido e Eneas. (Rio, 1953)
    Mágico, O. (Rio : Tempo Brasileiro, 1963; 28/2652)

Fontoura, Matheus da.
    Dindinha. In per. RTB, num. 259, j/f '51.

Fornari, Ernani.
    Nada! (Rio : Organização Simões, 1958; 23/5551)
    Quando se vive outra vez. In per. RTB, num. 235,
        maio '47.

Sem rumo. (Rio : Sociedade Brasileira de Autores
    Teatrais, 1951; 17/2647)
Sinha moça chorou. (São Paulo : Livr. Martins, 1941;
    7/4996)

Fornés, María Irene.
    Viuda, La. In anthol. 26/1881.

Fortes, Betty Yelda Brognoli Borges.
    Orfeu. (Canoas, Brazil : Editôra La Salle, 1963; 28/
    2653)

*França Júnior, Joaquim José da.
    Caiu o ministério. In anthol. 28/2656.
    Doutoras, As. (Rio : Sociedade Brasileira de Autores
        Teatrais, 1932)
    Maldita parentela. In per. RTB, num. 300, n/d '57.
    Meia hora de cynismo. (São Paulo : Teixeira, 1934)

Franco, Afonso Arinos de Melo.
    Dirceu e Marilia. (São Paulo : Livr. Martins, 1942;
    8/4318)

Freire Júnior, F. J.
    Luar de paquetá. (Rio : Sociedade Brasileira de Aut-
        ores Teatrais, 1952; 18/2816)

Fuente, Sindulfo de la.
    Ruedo de Calatrava, El. (México : Tenzontle, 1954;
    19/5157)

*Galich, Manuel.
    15 de septiembre. In coll. 15/2438.
    Belem, 1813. In coll. 15/2438.
    Carta a Su Ilustrísima, Una. In coll. 15/2438.
    De lo vivo a lo pintado. (Guatemala : Ministerio de
        Educación Pública, 1953; 19/5158); also in coll.
        12/2750.
    Ida y vuelta. (Guatemala : Tipografía Nacional, 1949;
        15/2439)
    M'hijo el bachiller. (Guatemala : Ministerio de Educa-
        ción Pública, 1953; 19/5159); also in coll. 12/2750
        and 0/35.
    Mugre, La. (Guatemala : Ministerio de Educación
        Pública, 1953; 19/5160); also in coll. 0/35.
    Papá-Natas. (Guatemala : Ministerio de Educación
        Pública, 1953; 19/5161); also in coll. 12/2750 and
        0/35.

Pescado indigesto, El. (La Habana : Casa de las Américas, 1961; 26/1856)
Tren amarillo, El. (Buenos Aires : Ediciones Transición, 1955)

Gallegos, Gerardo.
"Juancho" Gómez. (Caracas : Coop. de artes gráficas, 1936; 3/3327)

Gallegos, Rómulo.
Doncella, La. In coll. 21/4216.

Galli, Santiago.
Novia de Copenhague, Una. (Buenos Aires, 1960; 24/5613)

Gallo, Blas Raúl.
Cuando la huelga de los inquilinos. (Buenos Aires : Quetzal, 1959; 24/5614)

Gama, Jota.
Loucuras de mamãe. In per. RTB, num. 299, s/o '57.

Gamarra, Abelardo M.
Escenas del carnaval en Lima. In coll. 26/1857.
Escenas en la campiña. In coll. 26/1857.
Ir por lana y salir trasquilado. In coll. 26/1857.
Na codeo. In coll. 26/1857.
Ya vienen los chilenos. In coll. 26/1857.

Gamboa, Federico.
Entre hermanos. (México, 1944)
Venganza de la gleba, La. In anthol. 20/4234.

Gamboa, José Joaquin.
Alucinaciones. In coll. 0/36.
Caballero, la muerte y el diablo, El. In coll. 0/36.
Carne, La. In coll. 0/36.
Cuento viejo. In coll. 0/36.
Diablo tiene frio, El. (México : Gómez de la Puente, 1923); also in coll. 0/36.
Espíritus. In coll. 0/36.
Hogar, El. In coll. 0/36.
Mismo caso, El. In coll. 0/36.
Muerte, La. In coll. 0/36.
Revillagigedos, Los. (México : Nación, 1928); also in coll. 0/36.

Si la juventud supiera. In coll. 0/36.
Un día vendrá. In coll. 0/36.
Via crucis. (México : Nación, 1927); also in coll.
     0/36; also in anthol. 20/4234.

Gandolfi Herrero, Arístides see Yunque, Alvaro.

García Berlanga, Luis, jt. auth. see under Zavattini, Cesare.

García de Paredes, Carlos M.
     Minotauro, El. In coll. 28/2293.
     Qué angosta es la puerta. In coll. 28/2293.

García, Juan Agustín.
     Cuarterona, La. In coll. 20/4217.
     Del uno... al otro. (Buenos Aires : Espiasse, 1920);
          also in coll. 20/4217.
     Episodio bajo el terror, Un. In coll. 20/4217.
     Mundo de los snobs, El. In coll. 20/4217.

*García Ponce, Juan.
     Canto de los grillos, El. (México : Imp. Universitaria,
          1958; 22/5309)

*García Velloso, Enrique.
     24 horas dictador. In coll. 13/2231.
     Avelino Perdiguero. (Madrid : J. Amado, 1922)
     Cadena, La. In coll. 13/2231.
     Chiripa rojo, El. (Buenos Aires : Universidad de
          Buenos Aires, 1965)
     Copetin, El. (Buenos Aires : Argentores, 1939)
     Gabino el mayoral. In anthol. 21/4209.
     Gigoló. (Buenos Aires : Ediciones del Carro de Tespis,
          1960; 28/2294)
     Mamá Culepina. (Buenos Aires : Astrada, 1947); also
          in coll. 13/2231.

García Velloso, Enrique; Testena, Folco; and González Castillo, José.
     Conquistadores del desierto, Los. (Buenos Aires :
          Comisión nacional de cultura, 1944; 10/3678)

*Garro, Elena.
     Andarse por las ramas. In coll. 22/5310.
     Arbol, El. In per. RML, nueva época, 3/4, marzo/
          abril '63, p. 10-31 (28/2295)
     Encanto, tendajón mixto, El. In coll. 22/5310.

Hogar sólido, Un. In coll. 22/5310.
Mudanza, La. In per. UV/PH, 10, abril-junio '59,
    p. 263-274 (23/5322)
Perros, Los. In per. UNAM/UM, 19:7, marzo '65,
    p. 20-23 (28/2296)
Pilares de doña Blanca, Los. In coll. 22/5310.
Rey Mago, El. In coll. 22/5310.
Señora en su balcón, La. In anthol. 24/5644; also in
    per. UV/PH, 11, julio-sept. '59, p. 435-444
    (25/5323)
Ventura Allende. In coll. 22/5310.

Gavidia, Francisco Antonio.
    Cuento de marinos. (San Salvador : Impr. Nacional,
        1947; 13/2232)
    Princesa Citalá, La. (San Salvador : Nacional, 1946)
    Ursino. In per. REV. MIN. CULT. , v. 5, num. 17-
        18, julio-dic. '45, p. 67-109 (12/2751)

Gené, Juan Carlos.
    Herrero y el diablo, El. (Buenos Aires : Talía, 1957;
        22/5311)

Genta, Walter Homero.
    Ciudad de odio. In coll. 12/2752.
    Mar de sombras. In coll. 12/2752.
    Mundo de amor. In coll. 12/2752.
    Tierra de sangre. In coll. 12/2752.

*Ghiano, Juan Carlos.
    Narcisa Garay, mujer para llorar. (Buenos Aires :
        Talía, 1959; 24/5616)

Ghiraldo, Alberto.
    Alas. In coll. 12/2753.
    Alma gaucha. (Madrid : Renacimiento, 1921); also in
        coll. 12/2753.
    Andresito Vazquez (based on David Copperfield.) In
        coll. 12/2753.
    Café de Mamá Juana, El. In coll. 12/2753.
    Capitán Veneno (based on novel by Pedro Antonio de Al-
        arcón.) In coll. 12/2753.
    Columna de fuego, La. (Madrid, 1920); also in coll.
        12/2753.
    Copa de sangre, La. In coll. 12/2753.
    Cruz, La. In coll. 12/2753.
    Doña Modesta Pizarro. In coll. 12/2753.

Inmortal (based on Cadiz by Benito Pérez Galdós.)   In
   coll. 12/2753.
Ramona (based on novel by Helen Hunt Jackson.)   In
   coll. 12/2753.
Salvajes, Los.   (Madrid : La Mañana, 1921); also in
   coll. 12/2753.
Se aguó la fiesta.   In coll. 12/2753.

Gibson Parra, Percy.
   Esa luna que empieza.   In anthol. 14/2966 and 0/12.

Girbal, Gladys Teresa.
   Chúcara, La.   (Buenos Aires : Término, 1952; 18/
      2687)

Girón Cerna, Carlos.
   Ixquic.   (La Habana : Editorial Hermes, 1935)
   Y al tercer día. . . .   (Guatemala : Editorial del Minister-
      io de Educación Pública, 1952. ; 18/2688)

Godoy, Emma.
   Caín, el hombre.   (México : Abside, 1950; 16/2788)

Goicochea, Carlos and Cordone, Rogelio.
   Noches de carnaval.   (Buenos Aires : Ediciones del
      Carro de Tespis, 1961; 28/2297)

Golwarz, Sergio.
   Comedia para maridos, Una.   (México : B. Costa-Amic,
      1959; 23/5324)

*Gomes Dias, Alfredo.
   Invasão, A.   In coll. 26/2076.
   Pagador de promesas, O.   (Rio : Agir, 1961; 24/5799;
      also in English as Journey to Bahia, Washington:
      Brazilian American Cultural Institute, 1964; 28/
      2653a)
   Revolução dos beatos, A.   In coll. 26/2076.

*Gomes, Roberto.
   Casa fechada, A.   In per.   RTB, num. 239, set. '47.

Gonçalves Dias, Antônio.
   Leonor de Mendonça.   In per.   RTB, num. 340, j/a
      '64.

*Gondim Filho, Isaac.
   Conflito na consciência.   (Recife, 1951; 17/2648)

Grande estiagem, A.   (Rio, 1955)

Gonzaga, Armando.
    Flor dos maridos, A.   In per.   RTB, num. 271, j/f
      '53.
    Noivo do outro mundo, Um.   In per.   RTB, num. 231,
      j '47.
    Poder das massas, O.   In per.   RTB, num. 247,
      o/n '48.

González Arrili, Bernardo.
    Afincaos, Los.   (Buenos Aires : M. Lorenzo Rañó,
      1940); also in anthol. 24/5626.

*González Castillo, José.
    Entre bueyes no hay cornadas.   In anthol. 21/4209.
    Hermana mía.   (Buenos Aires : Editorial Claridad, 1925)
    Serenata, La.   In anthol.   24/5627.

González Castillo, José, jt. auth.   see under García Velloso,
    Enrique.

*González de Eslava, Fernán.
    Coloquio séptimo.   In anthol. 12/2768.

González, Ingrid.
    Gloria.   In anthol. 25/4571.

González Pacheco, Rodolfo.
    A contramano.   In coll. 0/37.
    Hermano Lobo.   (Buenos Aires, 1936); also in coll.
      0/37.
    Hijos del pueblo.   In coll. 0/37.
    Hombre de la plaza pública, El.   In anthol. 0/30.
    Inundación, La.   In coll. 0/37.
    Magdalena.   In coll. 0/37.
    Natividad.   In coll. 0/37.
    Sembrador, El.   In coll. 0/37.
    Víboras, Las.   In coll. 0/37; also in anthol. 24/5626.

González Paredes, Ramón.
    Dos agonías.   (Caracas : Editorial Universitaria, 1948)
    Ellos.   In coll. 0/38.
    Personaje rival, El.   In per.   CULT. U. , 54, marzo-
      abril '56, p. 41-60 (20/4218)
    Samuel.   In coll. 0/38.

*Gorostiza, Carlos.
    Pan de la locura, El.   (Buenos Aires : Talía, 1958;
        23/5325)
    Puente, El.   (Buenos Aires : El Junco, 1949; 15/2440,
        and Losange, 1954; 20/4219)
    Reloj de Baltasar, El.   (Buenos Aires : Losange, 1955;
        20/4220)

*Gorostiza, Celestino.
    Color de nuestra piel, El.   (México, 1953); also in
        anthol. 20/4234 and 24/5638.
    Columna social.   (México : Costa-Amic, 1956; 21/
        4217)
    Escombros del sueño.   (México : Letras de Mexico,
        1939)
    Malinche, La, o, la leña está verde.   In anthol. 23/
        5343.
    Nuevo paraíso, El.   (México : Contemporáneos, 1930);
        also in anthol. 23/5348
    Ser o no ser.   (México : Artes Gráficas, 1935)

*Gorostiza, Manuel Eduardo de.
    Contigo pan y cebolla.   (Boston : Ginn, 1922; also Mac-
        millan, 1923 and Houghton, 1953); also in coll. 21/
        4218.
    Don Dieguito.   In coll. 21/4218.
    Indulgencia para todos.   (México : UNAM, 1942,); also
        in coll. 21/4218.

Gramcko, Ida.
    Dama y el oso, La.   (México : Editorial Intercontinen-
        tal, 1959; 23/5326)
    Loma del ángel, La.   In coll. 26/1858.
    María Lionza.   (Barquisimeto, Venezuela : Editorial
        Nueva Segovia, 1955; 20/4221); also in coll. 26/
        1858.
    Mujer del Catey, La.   In coll. 26/1858.
    Penélope.   In coll. 26/1858.

*Guarnieri, Gianfrancesco.
    Eles não usam Black-tie.   In per. RTB, num. 307-
        309, jan-jun '59.

Guillén, Nicolás.
    Sangre es un mar enorme, La.   In anthol. 18/2698.

Guimarães, Antonio.
    O que êles querem.   In per. RTB, num. 243, jan '48.

Guimarães, Pinheiro.
> Historia de uma moça rica. <u>In</u> per. RTB, n/j '57.

Guizado, Rafael.
> Allegro. <u>In</u> coll. 0/41; <u>also in</u> per. REV. INDIAS,
> num. 99, sept. '47, p. 1-12 (13/2233)

Gurgel, Amaral.
> Rua nova. (Rio : Sociedade Brasileira de Autores
> Teatrais, 1952; 18/2817)

*Gutiérrez, Eduardo and Podestá, José.
> Juan Moreira. (Buenos Aires : Imp. de la Universi-
> dad, 1935; 1/2113); <u>also in</u> anthol. 22/5312.

Gutiérrez Hermosillo, Alfonso.
> Día de su muerte, El. <u>In</u> coll. 11/3331.
> Escala de Jacob, La. <u>In</u> coll. 11/3331.
> Justicia, señores, La. <u>In</u> coll. 11/3331.
> Sombra del Lázaro, La. <u>In</u> coll. 11/3331.

Guzmán Cruchaga, Juan.
> María Cenicienta, o La otra cara del sueño. (2nd ed. ;
> San Salvador : Ministerio de Cultura, 1959; 23/5327)

Harmony, Olga.
> Nuevo día. <u>In</u> per. UV/PH, 23, julio-sept. '62,
> p. 409-456 (26/1859)

*Heiremans, Luis Alberto.
> Abanderado, El. <u>In</u> coll. 26/1860.
> Jaula en el árbol, La. <u>In</u> per. UCC/FT, 4:13, 1. tri-
> mestre '57, p. 5-33 (22/5313)
> Moscas sobre el mármol. (Santiago : Nuevo Extremo,
> 1958; 23/5328)
> Versos de ciego. <u>In</u> coll. 26/1860.

Hernández, Fausto.
> Inventor del saludo, El. (Rosario : Ruiz, 1955; 19/
> 5162)

Hernández, Francisco Alfonso <u>see</u> Alfonso, Paco.

Hernández, Leopoldo.
> Pendiente, La. (La Habana : Tip. Ponsiano, 1959; 23/
> 5329)

*Hernández, Luisa Josefina.
    Agonía. (México, 1951)
    Arpas blancas, conejos dorados. In per. UV/PH, 2.
        época, 28, julio-sept. '63, p. 637-691 (28/2298)
    Calle de la gran ocasión, La. (Xalapa : Univ. Vera-
        cruzana, 1962; 28/2299)
    Clemencia. In per. INBA/CBA, 4:3, marzo '63, p. 61-
        80, and 4:4, abril '63, p. 65-92 (28/2300)
    Duendes, Los. In anthol. 28/2306; also in per. UV/
        PH, 14, abril-junio '60, p. 153-204 (25/4563)
    Frutos caídos, Los. In anthol. 20/4234 and 24/5638.
    Hija del rey, La. In anthol. 28/2301.
    Historia de un anillo. In per. UV/PH, 20, oct. -dic.
        '61, p. 693-740 (26/1861)
    Huéspedes reales, Los. (Xalapa : Univ. Verazruzana,
        1958; 22/5314)
    Sordomudos, Los. (México : América, 1953)

Hernández, Luisa Josefina, jt. auth. see under Carballido,
    Emilio.

*Herrera, Ernesto.
    León ciego, El. In anthol. 24/5640.

Herrera y Reissig, Julio.
    Adelfa. In coll. 26/1862.
    Sombra, La. In coll. 26/1862.

*Holanda, Nestor de.
    Um homen mau. (Rio : Ed. da revista Brasilidade,
        1942)

Ibarbourou, Juana de.
    Ascua de oro. In coll. 0/42.
    Boina roja. In coll. 0/42.
    Bruja y la molinera, La. In coll. 0/42.
    Burrita desorejada, La. In coll. 0/42.
    Campana imposible, La. In coll. 0/42.
    Caperucita roja. In coll. 0/42 and 11/3332.
    Dulce milagro, El. In coll. 0/42 and 11/3332.
    Mariquita de oro y Mariquita de pez. In coll. 0/42.
    Mensajeras del rey, Las. In coll. 0/42.
    Mirada maléfica, La. In coll. 0/42 and 11/3332.
    Opinión general, La. In coll. 0/42.
    Sueño de Natacha, El. In coll. 0/42 and 11/3332.
    Primera lección, La. In coll. 0/42.
    Silfos, Los. In coll. 0/42 and 11/3332.

*Ibargüenguitia, Jorge.
    Ante varias esfinges. In UV/PH, 15, julio-sept. '60,
       p. 131-171 (25/4564)
    Atentado, El. In anthol. 28/2285.
    Clotilde en su casa. In coll. 28/2302; also in anthol.
       20/4234.
    Pájaro en mano. In coll. 28/230 2.
    Susana y los jóvenes. In anthol. 24/5638.
    Viaje superficial, El. In coll. 28/2302; also in per.
       RML, nueva época, 12/15, jun-sep '60, p. 27-76.

Icaza, Jorge.
    Flagelo. (Quito : Sindicato de escritores y artistas,
       1936; 2/2665)

Iglesias, Luis see Iglezias, Luiz.

Iglezias, Luiz.
    Bicho do mato. (Rio : Valverde, 1945; 11/3444)
    Chuvas de verão. (Rio : Coelho, 1942)
    Fantoche (Rio : Sociedade Brasileira de Autores Teat-
       rais, 1933)
    Onde estás, felicidade? In per. RTB, num. 267,
       m/j '52.
    Ultimo Guilherme, O. (Rio : Coelho, 1938)

Iglezias, Luiz, jt. auth. see under Santos, Miguel.

*Imbert, Julio.
    Azor. In per. IJACI/C, 7:26, 3. entrega, '60,
       p. 56-63; 8:27, 1. entrega, '61, p. 66-73; 8:28, 2.
       entrega, '61, p. 64-69 (25/4565)
    Dente, El. (Buenos Aires : Losange, 1954; 19/5163)
    Noche más larga del año, La. In per. IJACI/C, 5:19,
       abr-jun '58, p. 45-55 23/5330

*Inclán, Federico S.
    Detrás de esa puerta. In anthol. 26/1882.
    Esfinge llamada Cordelia, Una. In anthol. 23/5343.
    Hidalgo. (México, 1953)
    Ventana, La. In anthol. 24/5643.

Innes-Gonzáles, Eduardo.
    Cuento de otoño. (Caracas : Tip. central, 1921); also
       in coll. 0/43.
    La de los claveles rojos. (Caracas : Imprenta nacional,
       1922); also in coll. 0/43.
    Mamá de Fifina, La. In coll. 0/43.

Saldo de cuentos, o Entre viejos camaradas. (Cara-
cas : Tip. america, 1924)
Virgen del Carmen, La. In coll. 7/4709.
Vivir para los demás. In coll. 7/4709.

Jaramillo Arango, Rafael.
Cita a las cuatro. In per. REV. INDIAS, v. 33,
num. 105, sep-oct '48 (14/2954)

Jardim, Luís Inácio de Miranda.
Isabel do sertão. (Rio : Olympio, 1959; 23/5552)

Jiménez, Miguel Angel.
Historia de una gota de agua. In anthol. 23/5318.

Jiménez Rueda, Julio.
Caída de las flores, La. (México : G. Sisniega,
1923)
Cándido Cordero, empleado público. (México : Nación,
1929)
Lo que ella no pudo prever. (México : Ed. Cultura,
1923); also in English as The unforeseen in per.
POET LORE, v. 35, num. 1, 1924, p. 1-42.
Silueta de humo, La. In anthol. 20/4234.
Tempestad sobre las cumbres. (México, 1923)

Jiménez, Wilfredo.
Pasión de Florencio Sánchez. (Buenos Aires : Losange,
1955)

Josseau, Fernando.
Prestamista, El. (Buenos Aires : Talía 1957; 21/4219)

Júnior, França see França Júnior, Joaquim José da.

Kelly, Celso.
Beleza perturba, A. In coll. 0/4.
Cínicos. In coll. 21/4328.
Espôsas acusam, As. In coll. 0/4.
Homem feliz, O. In coll. 0/4.
Nâo há amor sem romance. In coll. 0/4.
Nasceu uma mulher! In coll. 21/4328.
No céu é assim. In 0/4.
Sétimo dia. In 0/4.

*Kraly, Néstor.
Junio 16. In anthol. 26/1863.

Krimer, Jorge.
    Visiten el museo. In per.   TALIA, supl. , 4:25,
       p. 1-13 (28/2303)

*Laferrère, Gregorio de.
    Bajo la garra. In coll. 18/2690.
    Caramelos, Los. In coll. 0/5.
    Cuarto de hora, El; o, Los dos derechos. In coll. 0/5
       and 18/2690.
    Invisibles, Los. In coll. 18/2690.
    Jettatore. In coll. 18/2690 and 28/2304; also in anthol.
       0/11; also in per. ESCENA, nov. '20.
    Las de Barranco. (Buenos Aires : La Cultura Argen-
       tina, 1923; also Editorial Aranjo, 1939); also in
       coll. 0/5 and 18/2690.
    Locos de verano. (Buenos Aires : Emecé, 1944); also
       in coll. 0/5, 18/2690, 28/2304.

Lago, Mario, jt. auth. see under Wanderley, José.

Laguerre, Enrique A.
    Resentida, La. In anthol. 24/5639.

*Larreta, Antonio.
    Oficio de tinieblas. (Montevideo : Impr. Siglo Ilustrado,
       1954; 24/5617)

Larreta, Enrique Rodríguez.
    Clamor. In coll. 24/5618.
    Don Telmo. In coll. 24/5618.
    En la tela del sueño. In coll. 0/44, 24/5618, and 25/
       4566.
    Huerta, La. In coll. 24/5618 and 25/4566.
    Jerónimo y su almohada. (Buenos Aires : El Ateneo,
       1945); also in coll. 0/44, 0/45, and 25/4566.
    La que buscaba don Juan. (Buenos Aires : Sopena,
       1941); also in coll. 0/44, 0/46, 0/47, and 25/4566.
    Linyera, El. (Buenos Aires : J. Roldán, 1932; also
       Rosso, 1937; and Sopena, 1945; 11/3333); also in
       coll. 0/44, 10/3679, and 25/4566.
    Pasión de Roma. (Buenos Aires : Rosso, 1937; also
       Sopena, 1941); also in coll. 0/44, 10/3679, and
       25/4566.
    Santa María del Buen Aire. (Buenos Aires : Viau y
       Zona, 1936; also Rosso, 1937; also Sopena, 1940;
       also Emecé, 1944); also in coll. 0/44, 0/49, and
       25/4566; also in Italian as Santa Maria della Buon'
       Aria, Buenos Aires : Compagnia Italo-Argentina

d'Elettricità, 1936)
Venancio. In coll. 0/44, 24/5618, and 25/4566.

*Lasser, Alejandro.
    Catón en Utica. (Caracas : Grafolit, 1948; 14/2955)
    General Piar, El. (Caracas : Tall. Patria, 1946; 12/
        2754)

Lavardén, Manuel de.
    Siripo. In per. BOL; ESTUD; TEATRO, año 3, v. 3,
        num. 8, enero '45, p. 11-22 (11/3334)

Lazo, Agustín.
    Caso de Don Juan Manuel, El. (México : Atenea, 1948);
        also in anthol. 20/4234.
    Huella, La. (México : Sociedad General de Autores de
        México, 1945; also Atenea, 1947)
    Segundo imperio. (México : Ediciones Letras de México,
        1946); also in per. HIJO PRODIGO, año 3, v. 8,
        num. 25, abril '45, p. 44-59, and num. 26, mayo
        '45, p. 99-117 (11/3335)

*Leguizamón, Martiniano.
    Boceto campestre. In coll. 26/1864.
    Calandria. (New York, 1932); also in coll. 26/1864.
    Del tiempo viejo. In coll. 26/1864.

*Lehmann, Marta.
    Flagelados, Los. (Buenos Aires : Talía, 1961; 26/
        1865)
    Lázaro. (Buenos Aires : Losange, 1959; 25/4567)

Lermitte, Carlos.
    Agujas del reloj, La. (Montevideo : Ed. Surcos, 1954)
    Encima de la noria una estrella. (Montevideo :
        L. I. G. U. , 1946); also in per. UMIP/RN, año 8,
        v. 32, num. 96, dic. '45, p. 391-437, and año 9,
        v. 33, num. 97, en. '46, p. 94-134 (12/2755)
    Ku Klux Klan siglo XX. (Montevideo : Surcos, 1954)
    Noche que yo era sol, La. (Montevideo : Surcos, 1954)
    Terra purpúrea, La. (Montevideo : Surcos, 1954)

Lima, Benjamin.
    Venenos. In per. RTB, num. 244, m/a '48.

*Lima, Edy.
    Farsa da espôsa perfeita, A. In per. RTB, num. 315,
        m/j '60.

Lira, Miguel Nicolás.
    Carlota de México. (México : Fábula, 1944)
    Diablo volvió al infierno, El. (México : Fábula, 1946;
        12/2756)
    Linda. (México : Fábula, 1942)
    Vuelta a la tierra. (México : Fábula, 1940); also in
        anthol. 20/4234.

List Arzubide, Germán.
    Comino va a la huelga. (México : Dept. de Bellas
        Artes, 1935)
    Gallina de los huevos de oro, La. In anthol. 0/33.
    Nuevo diluvio, El. In coll. 0/50.
    Sombras, La. In coll. 0/50.
    Ultimo juicio, El. In coll. 0/50.

*Lizárraga, Andrés.
    Alto Perú. In coll. 26/1866.
    Carro eternidad, El. In coll. 26/1866.
    Color soledad, Un. In coll. 26/1866.
    Linares, Los. In coll. 26/1866; also in anthol. 0/11
        and 25/4568.
    Quiere usted comprar un pueblo? (Buenos Aires :
        Ediciones La Rosa Blindada, 1964; 28/2305)
    Santa Juana de América. (La Habana, 1960; 24/5619);
        also in coll. 26/1866.
    Sígamos con balances y confesiones. In coll. 26/1866.
    Tres jueces para un largosilencio. In coll. 26/1866.

Llanderas, Nicolás de las and Malfatti, Arnaldo M.
    Así es la vida. (Buenos Aires : Sociedad General de
        Autores de la Argentina, 1952); also in anthol. 23/
        5309.

Lontiel, Octavio.
    Como en Oriente. (Buenos Aires : Tor, 1936)
    Diana. (Buenos Aires : Oclon, 1952; 18/2691)
    Marionetas sobre el médano. (Buenos Aires : Oclon,
        1955)
    Selección oriental. (Buenos Aires : Viau y Zona, 1936)

Lopes Cardoso, A.
    Caftens, Os. In per. RTB, num. 310, j/a '59.

López Crespo, Iris de.
    Esto es la guerra! In coll. 13/2234.
    Estrellas en ascua. In coll. 13/2234.
    Regreso, El. In coll. 13/2234.

Sueño del maquí, El. In coll. 13/2234.

López Lorenzo, Manuel.
    Venganza feliz, Una. (México : Editorial Cultura, 1958;
      22/5316)

Louzada, Armando.
    Cortina sonora. (Rio : Ed. José Olympio, 1942; 8/
      4320)

Lozano García, Carlos, jt. auth. see under Lozano García,
    Lazaro.

Lozano García, Lázaro and Lozano García, Carlos.
    Al fin mujer. (México : Nación, 1927); also in anthol.
      20/4234.

Macau, Miguel A.
    Encina, La. In coll. 0/52 and 0/53.
    Fuerza incontrastable, La. In coll. 0/52 and 0/53.
    Herencia maldita, La. In coll. 0/52 and 0/53.
    Julián. In coll. 3/3328 and 16/2789.
    Justicia en la inconsciencia, La. In coll. 3/3328 and
      16/2789.
    Maternidad es amor. In coll. 0/51.
    Partida, La. In coll. 3/3328 and 16/2789.
    Soledad. In coll. 0/51.
    Triunfo de la vida, El. In coll. 0/52, 3/3328, and
      16/2789.

*Macedo, Joaquim Manuel de.
    Macaco da vizinha. In per. RTB, num. 312, n/d '59.
    Moreninha, A. In per. RTB, num. 312, n/d '59.
    Novo otelo, O. In anthol. 28/2656.
    Remissão dos pecados. In per. RTB, num. 301, j/f
      '58.

*Machado de Assis, Joaquim Maria.
    Caminho da porta, O. In coll. 0/7.
    Descantos. In coll. 0/7.
    Deuses de casaca, Os. In coll. 0/7.
    Lição de botanica. In coll. 0/7.
    Não consultes medico. In coll. 0/7.
    Protocollo, O. In coll. 0/7.
    Quasi ministro. In coll. 0/7.
    Tu, só tu, puro amor. In coll. 0/7.

Machado, Lourival.
    Raquel. In per. ANHEMBI, v. 1, num. 1, dez. '50,
        p. 100-116 (16/2917)

*Machado, Maria Clara.
    Boi e o burro no caminho de Belém, O. In coll. 21/
        4329.
    Bruxinha que era boa. In coll. 21/4329.
    Chapèuzinho vermelho, O. In coll. 21/4329.
    Pluft, o fantasminha. In coll. 21/4329.
    Rapto das cebolinhas, O. In coll. 21/4329.

Magalhães, Heloisa Helena.
    Grandinos em apuros. (Rio : Sociedade Brasileira de
        Autores Teatrais, 1944; 10/3915)

*Magalhães Júnior, Raymundo.
    Carlota Joaquina. (Rio : Serviço graph. do Ministerio
        da Educação e Saúde, 1939; 6/4403)
    Casamento no Uruguai. (Rio : Sociedade Brasileira de
        Autores Teatrais, 1943)
    Essa mulher é minha. (Rio : Gráfica N. S. de Fátima,
        1955)
    Familia Léro-Léro, A. (Rio : Sociedade Brasileira de
        Autores Teatrais, 1945; 11/3445); also in per.
        RTB, num. 233, marco '47.
    Fugir, casar ou morrer. In per. RTB, num. 315,
        m/j '60.
    Homem que fica, O. In coll. 5/3974; also in anthol.
        28/2654.
    Imperador galante, O. (Rio : Ed. Zélio Valverde,
        1946; 12/2941)
    Judeu, Um. (Rio : A Noite, 1939; 5/3975)
    Mulher que todos querem, A. In coll. 5/3974.
    Novas aventuras da familia Lero-Lero. In per. RTB,
        num. 270, n/d '52.
    Testa de ferro, O. (Rio : Sociedade Brasileira de
        Autores Teatrais, 1939)
    Trio em lá menor. (Rio : Sociedade Brasileira de
        Autores Teatrais, 1946; 12/2942)
    Vila rica. (Rio : Ed. Z. Valverde, 1945; 11/3446)

*Magalhães, Paulo de.
    Alvorada. (1942)
    Amor é cégo, O. In per. RTB, num. 222, abr/m/j
        '44.
    Aventuras de um rapaz feio. In coll. 0/54.

Chapeuzinho vermelho.   (1932); also in per.   RTB, num.
    265, j /f '52.
Chica-Bôa.   In coll. 0/54;   also in per.   RTB, num.
    237, julho '47.
Coração não envelhece, O.   In coll. 0/54.
Diabo enloqueceu, O.   (Rio : Sociedade Brasileira de
    Autores Teatrais, 1944; 12/2940)
Ditadora, A.   In coll. 0/54.
Feia.   (Rio : Sociedade Brasileira de Autores Teatrais,
    1941); also in coll. 0/54.
Gigana me enganou, A.   In coll. 0/54.
Homem que salvou o Brasil, O.   (1931)
Loucuras do imperador.   (Rio : Editôra Talmagráfica,
    1952)
Marido da deputada, O.   (1952)
Preco da glória, O.   (1940)
Princesinha de Ouro, A.   In per.   RTB, num. 310,
    j /a '59.
Resignação!   (Rio : Livraria Cruz Coutinho, 1920)
Rio das mortes.   (1956)
Saudade.   (Rio : Sociedade Brasileira de Autores Teat-
    rais, 1934); also in coll. 0/54; also in per.   RTB,
    num. 256, m /j '50.
Simplicio pacáto.   (Rio : Sociedade Brasileira de Au-
    tores Teatrais, 1939)
Vícios modernos.   (Rio, 1922)

*Magaña, Sergio.
    Moctezuma II.   In per.   PANOR. TEAT. MEX. , 1:1,
        julio '54, p. 35-82 (20/4222)
    Pequeño caso de Jorge Lívido, El.   In anthol. 23/5343.
    Signos del zodíaco, Los.   (México : Editorial Intercon-
        tinental, 1953; 19/5165); also in anthol. 20/4234.

Magaña, Sergio, jt. auth.   see under Carballido, Emilio.

Magdaleno, Mauricio.
    Emiliano Zapata.   In coll. 0/99.
    Pánuco 137.   In coll. 0/99; also in anthol. 20/4234.
    Trópico.   In coll. 0/99.

*Maggi, Carlos.
    Apuntador, El.   In coll. 28/2307.
    Biblioteca, La.   In coll. 28/2308
    Cuervo en la madrugada, Un.   In coll. 28/2307.
    Noche de los ángeles inciertos, La.   In coll. 28/2307.
    Trastienda, La.   In coll. 28/2308.

*Malfatti, Arnaldo M. , jt. auth.   see under Llanderas, Nic-
olás de las.

Mallea, Eduardo.
 Gajo de enebro, El.   (Buenos Aires : Emecé, 1957;
  21/4220)
 Representación de los aficionados, La.   (Buenos Aires :
  Editorial Sudamericana, 1962; 28/2309.

Manceaux, Alberto.
 Angel, Un.   (Buenos Aires : Imp. López, 1946; 12/
  2757)
 Barón de Meda de Mouros, El.   (Buenos Aires : Cant-
  iello, 1946; 12/2758)
 Juicio de Paris, El.   (Buenos Aires, 1947)
 Sandra Machado.   (Buenos Aires : Cantiello, 1946; 12/
  2760)
 Ultima Dieguez, La.   (Buenos Aires : Imp. Lopez,
  1946; 12/2761)
 Un joker y cuatro reinas.   (Buenos Aires : Cantiello,
  1946; 12/2759)

Manco, Silveiro.
 Juan Moreira.   In anthol. 0/89.

Manet, Eduardo.
 Infanta que no quiso tener ojos verdes, La.   In coll.
  15/2441.
 Presagio.   In coll. 15/2441.
 Scherzo.   In coll. 15/2441.

*María, Enrique de.
 Bohemia criolla.   In anthol. 24/5627.

Maria Jacintha   see Trovão da Costa, Maria Jacintha.

*Marín, Gerard Paul.
 En el principio la noche era serena.   In anthol. 25/
  4582.

Marín, Juan.
 Emperador Kwang hsü, El.   (Tokio : Asia América,
  1941)
 Orestes y yo.   (Tokio : Asia-América, 1940; 6/4157.
  Also in English as Orestes and I, same publ. ,
  1940)

*Marqués, René.
    Apartamento, El. In anthol. 28/2292.
    Carreta, La. (Rio Piedras : Editorial Cultura, 1961;
        24/5620); also in anthol. 26/1883; also in per.
        UPRAG/A, 7:4, oct-dic '51, p. 67-87; 8:1, en-mar
        '52, p. 54-78; 8:3, jul-sep. '52, p. 66-92 (18/
        2692)
    Casa sin reloj, La. (Xalapa : Univ. Veracruzana,
        1962; 25/4569)
    Hombre y sus sueños, El. In per. UPRAG/A, 4:4,
        num. 2, abr-jun '48, p. 58-72 (14/2956)
    Juan Bobo y la dama de occidente. (México : Los
        Presentes, 1956; 21/4221)
    Mariana, o, El alba. (Villa Nevares, Cuba, 1965; 28/
        2310)
    Muerte no entrará en palacio, La. In coll. 23/5331;
        also in anthol. 28/2388b.
    Niño azul para esa sombra, Un. In coll. 23/5331;
        also in anthol. 25/4582.
    Sol y los Macdonald, El. (San Juan, 1950); also in
        per. UPRAG/A, 13:1, en-mar '57, p. 43-82 (21/
        4222)
    Soles truncos, Los. In coll. 23/5331; also in anthol.
        23/5344.

*Martí, José.
    Abdala. In coll. 0/56.
    Adúltera. (La Habana : El Trópico, 1936; 2/2666)
    Amor con amor se paga. In coll. 0/56.

Martínez Cuitiño, Vicente.
    Cuervos rubios. In coll. 0/59.
    Derrumbe, El. In coll. 0/58 and 0/59.
    Diamantes quebrados. (Buenos Aires : Argentores,
        1934)
    Fuerza ciega, La. In coll. 0/57.
    Humilde quimera, La. In coll. 0/57.
    Mala siembra, La. In coll. 0/58 and 0/59.
    Mate dulce. In coll. 0/59.
    Nuevo mundo. In coll. 0/58 and 0/59.
    Noche del alma. (Buenos Aires : Argentores, 1947)
    Servidumbre. (Buenos Aires : Tespis, 1958); also in
        anthol. 24/5640.
    Superficie. (Buenos Aires : Argentores, 1934)

Martínez Estrada, Ezequiel.
    Cazadores. In coll. 22/5318.

Lo que no vemos morir.   (Buenos Aires : Conducta,
   1941); also in coll. 22/5318.
Sombres.   In coll. 22/5318.

*Martínez, José de Jesús.
   Aurora y el mestizo.   (Panamá : Ediciones del Depart-
      amento de Bellas Artes, 1964)
   Juicio final.   In anthol. 28/2388b.
   Perrera, La.   In coll. 0/60.
   Venganza, La.   In coll. 0/60.

Masip, Paulino.
   Dúo.   In per.   RUECA, año 4, num. 14, primavera
      '44, p. 16-25 (11/3336)
   Emplazado, El.   (México : Sociedad General de Au-
      tores de México, 1949)
   Frontera, La.   (Madrid, 1933)
   Hombre que hizo un milagro, El.   (México : Editor-
      ial Atlante, 1944)

Martorras Cornejo, Carlos.
   Escaparate, El.   In coll. 18/2693.
   Zeus está ausente.   In coll. 18/2693.

Maturana, José de.
   Flor del trigo, La.   In anthol. 24/5626.

*Medina, Roberto Nicolás.
   Cuatro paredes, Las.   In anthol. 24/5612.

Mediz Bolio, Antonio.
   Fuerza de los débiles, La.   In coll. 22/5319.
   Ola, La.   In coll. 22/5319.

*Méndez Ballester, Manuel.
   Clamor de los surcos, El.   (San Juan : Baldrich, 1940);
      also in coll. 0/61.
   Encrucijada.   (San Juan, 1958; 23/5332); also in anthol.
      23/5344.
   Feria, La.   In anthol. 28/2291.
   Hilarion.   (San Juan, 1943)
   Milagro, El.   In anthol. 26/1883.
   Misterio del castillo, El.   (San Juan, 1946)
   Tiempo muerto.   (San Juan : Baldrich, 1940); also in
      coll. 0/61; also in anthol. 28/2290.

Mendoza Gutiérrez, Alfredo.

Juan Pobre y los cuatro ladrones. In coll. 24/5621.
Muertos resucitados, Los. In coll. 24/5621.
Noche de difuntos. In coll. 24/5621.

Mendoza, Héctor.
    Camelia, La. In per. UNAM/UM, 13:10, jun. '59,
        p. 13-15 (23/5333)
    Cosas simples, Las. (México : Librería Studium,
        1954; 19/5166); also in anthol. 20/4234.

*Menéndez, Roberto Arturo.
    Ira del cordero, La. (San Salvador : Ministerio de
        Cultura, 1959; 23/5334)
    Nuevamente Edipo. (San Salvador : Ministerio de Edu-
        cación, 1966)

Mesquita, Alfredo.
    Casa assombrada. (São Paulo, 1938)
    Em familia. (São Paulo, 1937); also in coll. 0/62.
    Esperança de familia, A. In coll. 0/62.
    Gran-fina. In coll. 0/62.
    Noite de S. João. (São Paulo, 1936)
    Priâmidas, Os. (Rio : José Olympio, 1942; 9/4296)
    Retours. (Rio : José Olympio, 1942)

Messina, Felipe.
    Felicidade chegou, A. (Rio, 1943)
    Homens!--Que horror!, Os. (Rio : Coelho, 1943; 9/
        4297)

Meyrialle, Horacio S.
    Todo el año es navidad. (Buenos Aires : Ediciones
        Mariel, 1960; 24/5622)

*Milanés, José Jacinto.
    A buena hambre no hay pan duro. In coll. 28/2312.
    Conde Alarcos, El. In coll. 28/2312.
    Miron Cubano, El. In coll. 28/2312.
    Poeta en la corte, Un. In coll. 28/2312.
    Por el puente o por el río. In coll. 28/2312.

Milanez, Abdon.
    Centelha, A. In per. RTB, num. 251, m/j '49.

Miró, César, and Salazar Bondy, Sebastián.
    Ollantay (adaptation). (Lima : Mar del Sur; also Lib-
        rería Internacional del Perú, 1963; 28/2321)

*Molleto Enrique.
    Cambio importante, Un. In coll. 24/5623.
    Llamada, La. In coll. 24/5623.
    Sóltano, El. (Santiago : Sociedad de Escritores de
        Chile, 1963; 28/2313)
    Telescopio, El. In coll. 24/5623.
    Torre, La. (Santiago : Editorial del Pacífico, 1961;
        26/1867)

*Mombrú, María.
    Andén, El. In coll. 25/4570.
    Juan Esteban. In coll. 25/4570.
    Maquillaje. In coll. 25/4570.
    Señoritas vecinas, Las. In anthol. 26/1863.

Mondragón Aguirre, Magdalena.
    Cuando Eva se vuelve Adán. In coll. 13/2235.
    Mundo perdido, El. In coll. 0/63.
    No debemos morir. (León : Editorial Moderna, 1944)
    Porque me da la gana! (México, 1953)
    Sirena que llevaba el mar, La. (México : Unión Nacion-
        al de Autores, 1951); also in coll. 0/63.
    Torbellino. In coll. 13/2235.

*Montaine, Eliseo.
    Don Rufo de los milagros. (Buenos Aires : Talía, 1960;
        25/4568); also in anthol. 0/11.
    Mujeres en el desierto. (Buenos Aires : Argentores,
        1946)

Montaine, Eliseo, jt. auth. see under Tálice, Roberto Ale-
    jandro.

*Montalvo, Juan.
    Descomulgado, El. (Ambato : Tip. Coegio Bolívar,
        1931); also in coll. 1/2116.
    Dictador, El. In coll. 1/2116; also in per. UNIV.
        HABANA, v. 3, num. 7, 1935, p. 49-66 (1/2115)
    Granja. In coll. 1/2116.
    Leprosa, La. In coll. 1/2116.

*Monteiro, Jose Maria.
    Prima Donna. In per. RTB, num. 296, m/a '57.

Montello, Josué.
    Baronesa, A. (Rio : Olympio, 1960; 23/5553)
    Miragem, A. (Rio : Olympio, 1959; 23/5554)

Verdugo, O.   (Rio : Gráfica Olímpica Editôra, 1954;
    19/5353)

Monterde, Francisco.
    Careta de cristal, La.   (México : Sociedad General de
        Autores de México, 1948)
    En el remolino.   (México : Ediciones de la revista An-
        tena, 1924)
    La que volvió a la vida.   (México : Nación, 1926); also
        in English as She who returned to life in per.   POET
        LORE, v. 55, num. 4, Winter '50, p. 291-335.
    Oro negro.   (México : Nación, 1927)
    Proteo.   (México, 1931; also Editora Intercontinental,
        1944); also in anthol. 20/4234.

Montero, Marco Antonio.
    Puerta de oro, La.   In per.   UV/PH, 2. época, 3,
        jul-sep. '57. p. 85-96 (28/2314)

*Montes Huidobro, Matías de.
    Tiro por la culata, El.   In anthol. 25/4571.

Moock Bousquet, Armando.
    Cancionero del niño, El.   (Santiago : Cultura, 1937)
    Crimen en mi pueblo, Un.   (Santiago : Cultura, 1936)
    Cuando venga el amor.   (Santiago : Nascimento, 1929);
        also in coll. 3/3329.
    Del brazo y por la calle.   (Buenos Aires : Argentores,
        1939; also Madrid : Gráficas Arba, 1948)
    Mocosita.   (Buenos Aires, 1929)
    Mundial pantomim.   In coll. 0/64.
    Natacha.   In coll. 0/64.
    Pueblecito.   (Santiago : Nascimento, 1929); also in coll.
        3/3329.
    Rigoberto.   (Buenos Aires : Argentores, 1935; also
        Boston : Heath, 1954)
    Señorita Charleston.   In coll. 0/64.
    Serpiente, La.   In coll. 3/3329; also in anthol. 20/
        4201.

*Mora, Juan Miguel de.
    Primero es la luz.   (México : Helio-México, 1955; 19/
        5167)

Moraes, Marcus Vinicius de Melo.
    Orfeu da conceição.   (Rio : Liv. São José, 1960; 25/
        4726)

Moreno, Gloria.
  Ultima victoria, La. (Santiago : Zig-Zag, 1945; 11/
    3337)

Moreno, Luis.
  Medianoche en la tierra. In anthol. 28/2301.
  Sueños encendidos, Los. In anthol. 23/5343.

Morisseau-Leroy, Félix.
  Antigone en créole. (Pétion-ville, Haiti : Culture,
    1953; 22/5582)

Mota, Fernando.
  Como ve el hombre a la mujer al paso de los años.
    In coll. 24/5624.
  Llave, La. In coll. 24/5624.
  María de Magdala. (México : Unión Nacional de Au-
    tores, 195?)
  Muerte en el convento, La. In coll. 24/5624.
  Trucos de Maese Pedro, Los. In coll. 24/5624.
  Ultimo Werther, El. In coll. 24/5624.

*Nalé Roxlo, Conrado.
  Cola de la sirena, La. (Buenos Aires : Hachette,
    1941); also in coll. 21/4223; also in anthol. 23/
    5309.
  Cuervo del arca, El. In coll. 11/3337.
  Judith y las rosas. In coll. 21/4223.
  Neblí, El. In coll. 28/2315.
  Pacto de Cristina, El. In coll. 11/3338 and 21/4223.
  Pasado de Elisa, El. In coll. 28/2315.
  Reencuentro, El. In coll. 28/2315.
  Vacío, El. In coll. 28/2315.
  Viuda difícil, Una. (Buenos Aires : Poseidon, 1944;
    also New York : Norton, 1953); also in coll. 21/
    4223.

Nascimento, Abdias do.
  Sortilégio. In per. ANEHMBI, año 3, 12:36, nov. '53,
    p. 544-565 (19/5354)

Navarrete, Rodolfo.
  Mago, El. (Buenos Aires : Losange, 1957; 22/5320)

*Neto, Coêlho.
  Patinho torto, O; ou, Os misterios do sexo. In per.
    RTB, num. 341, s/o '64.
  Quebranto. In per. RTB, num. 295, j/f '57.

Noriega Hope, Carlos.
    Señorita voluntad, La.   (México : Nación, 1927); also in
        anthol. 20/4234.

*Novión, Alberto.
    Barbijo, El.   (Buenos Aires : Argentores, 1952)
    Bendita seas.   (Buenos Aires : Argentores, 1934)
    Chusma, La.   (Buenos Aires : Quetzal, 1957; 21/4224)
    En un burro tres baturros.   (Buenos Aires : Argentores,
        1955)
    Fonda de Pacarito, La.   In anthol. 21/4209.

*Novo, Salvador.
    A ocho columnas.   (México : Stylo, 1956; 21/4225)
    Coronel Astucias y los hermanos de la hoja, o, Los
        charros contrabandistas.   (México : INBA, 1948;
        14/2957)
    Cuautémoc.   (México, 1962; 28/2316); also in coll. 28/
        2318.
    Culta dama.   La.   (México : Impresora Veracruz, 1951;
        17/2559); also in anthol. 20/4234.
    Diálogo de ilustres.   In coll. 28/2318.
    Don Quijote en las escena.   (México : INBA, 1948; 14/
        2958); also in per.   MEX ARTE, num., 1, jul '48
        (14/2959)
    Guerra de las gordas, La.   (México : Fondo de Cultura
        Económica, 1963; 28/2317); also in anthol. 28/2306.
    Ha vuelto Ulises.   (México : Ediciones Era, 1962; 26/
        1868)
    In Ticitezcatl, o, El espejo encantado.   In coll. 28/
        2318.
    Joven II, El.   (México, 1951; 17/2560)
    Malinche y Carlota.   In anthol. 24/5643.
    Sofá, El.   In coll. 28/2318; also in per.   INBA/CBA,
        4:8, agosto '63, p. 53-92 (28/2319)
    Tercero Fausto, El.   (In French as Le troisième
        Faust. Paris, 1934)
    Yocasta, o, Casi.   (México : Textos de la Capilla,
        1961; 24/5625)

Nunes, Mario.
    Frutos da época.   In per.   RTB, num. 278, m/a '54.

Ocampo, María Luisa.
    Al otro día.   In anthol. 20/4234.
    Cosas de la vida.   (México : Nación, 1926)

Olivari, Carlos, jt. auth.   see under   Pondal Ríos, Sixto.

Olivari, Nicolás.
    Seca, La. (Buenos Aires : ENE, 1955; 19/5168)
    Tedio. (Buenos Aires : Tespis, 1964; 28/2320)

Oliveira e Silva, Francisco.
    Homem diferente, Um. In per. RTB, num. 253, o/n/
        d '49.

Oliveira, Jocy de.
    Apague meu spotlight. (São Paulo : Massao Ohno Edi-
        tôra, 1962; 26/2078)

*Oliveira, Valdemar de.
    Mulher inteligente, Uma. In per. RTB, num. 249, j/
        f '49.

Oliveira, Valdemar de and Borba Filho, Hermilo.
    Soldados da retaguarda. (Recife, 1945)

Olmedo López, Eduardo.
    Casa de Mariana, La. (La Paz : Alcaldía Municipal,
        1958; 22/5321)

Ordóñez, Eduardo.
    Por encima de todo. (La Habana : Lex, 1953; 19/5169)

Orgambide, Pedro G.
    Concierto para caballero solo. (Buenos Aires : Editor-
        ial Stilcograf, 1963; 23/2322)

Orlando, Paulo.
    Cabelereiro de minha mulher, O. (Rio : Sociedade
        Brasileire de Autores Teatrais, 1951)
    Crime do libório, O. (Rio : Sociedade Brasileira de
        Autores Teatrais, 1945; 12/2943)
    Leilão da felicidade. (Rio : Sociedade Brasileira de
        Autores Teatrais, 1943)
    Maridos atacan de madrugada, Os. In RTB, num. 238,
        ag. '47.
    Se o Anacleto soubesse. (Rio : Sociedade Brasileira de
        Autores Teatrais, 1934): also in per. RTB, num.
        258, '50.

Orosa Díaz, Jaime.
    Se vende un hombre. (Mérida : Univ. Nacional del
        Sureste, 1956; 20/4223)

Orrego Vicuña, Eugenio.
    Alba de oro, El. In per. UCH/A, ser. 3, año 99,
        num. 41, '41, p. 46-192.
    Amigo de Hamlet, El. In coll. 14/2960.
    Amo de su alma, El. (Santiago : Chile Nuevo, 1924)
    Camino adelante. (Santiago : Prensas de la Universidad
        de Chile, 1941)
    Carrera. (Santiago : Prensas de la Universidad de
        Chile, 1933)
    Catalina Isabel. In coll. 14/2960.
    En el umbral. In coll. 14/2960.
    Lobo, El. (Santiago : Nascimento, 1933)
    Niña sonrisa, La. In coll. 14/2960.
    Noche de San Silvestre. In coll. 14/2960.
    Rechazada, La. (Santiago : Editorial Hispánica, 1923)
    Reino sin término, El. (Santiago : Prensas de la Uni-
        versidad de Chile, 1946)
    San Martín. (Santiago : Ed. Cultura, 1938)
    Tragedia interior. (Santiago, 1925)
    Vírgenes modernas. (Santiago : Imprenta Universitaria,
        1930)

Orteiza, Alberto M.
    Doctora Dosset, La. (Buenos Aires : Olimpo, 1954)
    Y yo soy el héroe! (La Plata : Municipalidad de La
        Plata, 1962; 26/1869)

Ortíz de Montellano, Bernardo.
    Sombrerón, El. (México : La Estampa Mexicana, 1946;
        12/2762)

Ortiz Guerrero, Manuel.
    Conquista, La. (Asunción : Editorial Paraguaya, 1926);
        also in coll. 0/65.
    Crimen de Tintalida, El. In coll. 0/65.
    Eireté. (Villarica, 1921); also in coll. 0/65.

*Osorio, Luis Enrique.
    Ahí sos, camisón rosao! In coll. 28/2323.
    Al amor de los escombros. (Buenos Aires, 1922); also
        in coll. 28/2323.
    Aspasia, Cortesana de Mileto. In coll. 28/2323.
    Bombas a domicilio. In coll. 28/2323.
    Cantar de la tierra, El. In coll. 28/2323.
    Creadores, Los. In coll. 28/2323.
    Doctor Manzanillo, El. (Bogotá, 1943)
    Entre cómicos te has de ver. In coll. 28/2323.
    Espíritus andan sueltos, Los. In coll. 28/2323.

Familia política, La. In coll. 28/2323.
Hombre que hacía soñar, El. (Bogotá, 1946)
Iluminado, El. (Barranquilla : Novela Semanal, 1929;
    also Minerva, 1936); also in coll. 28/2323.
Imperfecta casada, La. In coll. 28/2323.
Loco de moda, El. In coll. 28/2323.
Manzanillo en el poder. (Bogotá : La Idea, 1945; 11/
    3339)
Nube de abril. In coll. 28/2323.
Nudo ciego. (Bogotá, 1943)
Pájaros grises. In coll. 28/2323.
Paro femenino. In coll. 28/2323.
Préstame tu marido. In coll. 23/2323.
Que tu esposa no lo sepa. In coll. 28/2323.
Rajá de pasturacha, El. In coll. 28/2323.
Rancho ardiendo. In coll. 28/2323.
Ruta inmortal, La. In coll. 28/2323.
Se fuga una mujer. In coll. 28/2323.
Sed de justicia. (Bogotá : Cromos, 1921)
Sí, mi teniente. In coll. 28/2323.
Toque de queda. In coll. 28/2323.
Tragedia íntima. (Bogotá, 1944); also in coll. 28/2323.
Zar de precios, El. In coll. 28/2323.

Othón, Manuel José.
    Después de la muerte. In coll. 0/66.
    Lo que hay detrás de la dicha. In coll. 0/66.
    Ultimo capitulo, El. In coll. 0/66; also in anthol. 20/
        4234.

Ozores, Renato.
    Angel, Un. In coll. 0/67.
    Fuga, La. (Panamá : Ministerio de Educación, 1959;
        23/5335)
    Mujer desconocida, Una. In coll. 0/67.

*Pacheco, Carlos Mauricio.
    Arroyo maldonado, El. In per. ENTREACTO, año 1,
        num. 11, jun '22.
    Barracas. In anthol. 24/5627.
    Boca del riachuelo, La. In per. ESCENA, año 8,
        num. 350, mar. '25.
    De hombre a hombre. In per. TEAT NAC, año 3,
        num. 133, nov. '20.
    Disfrazados, Los. (Buenos Aires : Quetzal, 1954)
    Don Quijano de la Pampa. In coll. 0/68.
    Equilibristas, Los. (Buenos Aires : Argentores, 1936)
    Fuertes, Los. In coll. 0/68.

Guardia del auxiliar, La. In per. ESCENA, año 9,
   num. 398, enero '26.
Mazorca, La. In per. ESCENA, año 8, num. 345,
   feb. '25.
Morisqueta final, La. In per. ESCENA, año 10, en. '27.
Otro mundo, El. In per. ENTREACTO, año 1, num.
   4, 1922.
Ribera, La. In anthol. 21/4209; also in per. TEAT
   ARG, año 2, num. 31, 1920.
Romerias, Las. In per. TEAT ARG, año 2, num. 31,
   1920.
Ropa vieja. In per. ESCENA, año 6, sup. num. 84,
   jul '23.
Tierra del fuego, La. In per. ESCENA, año 6, num.
   248, mar. '23.
Veinte años después. In per. TEAT POP, año 3, num.
   72, mar. '29, 1921.

Páez, Leonardo.
   Bruma frente al espejo, La. In coll. 22/5322.
   Lluvia de verano. In coll. 22/5322.

*Pagano, José León.
   Cartas de amor. (Buenos Aires : Moro, Tello & Cia.,
      1921)
   Día de la ira, El. (Buenos Aires : Poseidon, 1959;
      24/2628)
   Rescate, El. (Buenos Aires : Argentores, 195?)
   Secreto, El. In anthol. 23/5309.
   Venganza de Afrodite, La. (Buenos Aires : Alba, 1954)
   Zarpazo, El. (Buenos Aires : Argentores, 195?); also
      in coll. 0/69.

Pagés Larraya, Antonio.
   Santos Vega, el payador. (Buenos Aires : Ediciones
      Doble P, 1953; 19/5170)

*Palant, Pablo.
   Días del odio, Los. (Buenos Aires : Argentores, 1946)
   Dicha impía, La. (Buenos Aires : Tespis, '57; 22/5323)
   Escarabajo, El. (Buenos Aires : Talía, 1962; 23/2324)

Palino, Piquio.
   Divina tragedia, La. In coll. 23/5336.
   Maestros cantores, Los. In coll. 23/5336.
   Ocaso de la diosa, El. In coll. 23/5336.

Paolantonio, Jorge M.

Siete jefes. <u>In</u> anthol. 26/1863.

*Paoli, Carlos de.
    Velorio del Angelito, El. <u>In</u> anthol. 21/4209.

Parada León, Ricardo.
    Dolor de los demás, El. (México : Sociedad General de
        Autores de México, 194?)
    Esclava, La. (Madrid : La Nación, 1927)
    Hacia la meta. <u>In</u> anthol. 20/4234.

Paredes, Margarita V. de.
    Historia de caracoles. <u>In</u> anthol. 23/5318.

*Parrado, Gloria.
    Paz en el sombrero, La. <u>In</u> anthol. 26/1881.

*Pasos, Joaquin and Coronel Urtecho, José.
    Chinfonía burguesa. <u>In</u> anthol. 23/5346.

Patrón, Juan Carlos.
    Procesado 1040. (Buenos Aires : Losange, '57; 22/5324)

*Payró, Roberto J.
    Alegría. (Buenos Aires : Imprenta de la Universidad,
        1936); <u>also in</u> coll. 20/4224.
    Canción trágica. (Buenos Aires : Minerva, 1929); <u>also</u>
        <u>in</u> coll. 20/4224; also in English as The tragic song
        <u>in</u> per. POET LORE, v. 50, num. 1, Spring '44.
    Cartera de justicia, La. In per. BOL ESTUD TEAT-
        RO, año 4, v. 4, num. 12, mar '46, p. 38-54
        (12/2763)
    Fuego en el rastrojo. <u>In</u> coll. 0/70 and 20/4224.
    Marco Severi. (Buenos Aires : Comisión nacional de
        cultura, 1946; 12/2764); <u>also in</u> coll. 20/4224;
        <u>also in</u> per. ESCENA, año 3, num. 88, mar. '20.
    Mientraiga. <u>In</u> coll. 0/70 and 20/4224.
    Sobre las ruinas. (Buenos Aires : Bambalinas, 1920;
        also Boston : Heath, 1943; 9/3949); <u>also in</u> coll.
        20/4224.
    Triunfo de los otros, El. <u>In</u> coll. 20/4224.
    Vivir qiero conmigo. <u>In</u> coll. 0/70 and 20/4224.

*Paz, Octavio.
    Hija de Rappacini, La. In anthol. 23/5348; <u>also in</u> per.
        RML, 1:7, sep-oct. '56, p. 3-26 (20/4225)

Pederneiras, Raul.
    Chá do Sabugueiro, O. <u>In</u> per. RTB, num. 261, m/j '51.

Pederneiras, Raul and Peixoto, Luiz.
Amor e Mêdo. In per. RTB, num. 237, jul '47.

Peixoto, Luiz.
Paixão, A. In per. RTB, num. 279, m/j '54.

Peixoto, Luiz and Bettencourt, Carlos.
Forrobodó. In per. RTB, num. 322, j/a '61 (28/
2655)

Peixoto, Luiz, jt. auth. see under Pederneiras, Raul.

Peixoto, Maria Luiza Amaral.
Dilema, O. In coll. 25/4727.
Velório amigo. In coll. 25/4727.
Volta do barão, A. In coll. 25/4727.

Pellegrini, Aldo.
Buscadora de amor, La. In 28/2325.
Cinco divirtimientos. In coll. 28/2325.
Escalera, La. In coll. 28/2325.

Pena, Martins see Penna, Luíz Carlos Martins.

Penna, Luíz Carlos Martins.
Bolingbrok & Cia, ou, As casadas solteiras. In coll.
22/5527; also in per. RTB, num. 248, dec. '48.
Caixeiro da taverna, O. In coll. 0/71, 0/98, 9/4298,
22/5527, 25/4728.
Cigano, O. In coll. 22/5527.
D. João de Lira, ou, O repto. In coll. 22/5527.
D. Leonor Teles. In coll. 22/5527.
Diletante, O. In coll. 0/71, 9/4298, and 22/5527.
Dous, Os, ou, O inglês Maquinista. In coll. 0/71,
9/4298, and 22/5527.
Drama sem título. In coll. 22/5527.
Família e a festa da roça, A. In coll. 0/71, 9/4298,
and 22/5527.
Fernando, ou, O cinto acusador. In coll. 22/5527.
Irmãos das almas, Os. In coll. 0/71, 0/98, 9/4298,
22/5527, and 25/4728.
Itaminda, ou, O guerreiro de Tupã. In coll. 22/5527.
Judas em sábado de aleluia, O. In coll. 0/71, 0/98,
9/4298, 17/2649, 22/5527, 25/4728; also in anthol.
28/2656.
Juiz de paz da roça, O. In coll. 0/71, 0/98, 9/4298,
17/2649, 22/5527, 25/4728.

Meirinhos, Os. In coll. 22/5527.
Namorador, O, ou A noite de S. João. In coll. 22/
5527.
Noviço, O. (São Paulo, 1948); also in coll. 0/98, 9/
4298, 22/5527, and 25/4728.
Quem casa quer casa. In coll. 0/71, 0/98, 9/4298,
22/5527, and 25/4728.
Sertanejo na côrte, Um. In coll. 22/5527.
Três médicos, Os. In coll. 22/5527.
Vitiza ou, O Nero de Espanha. In coll. 22/5527.

*Peón y Contreras, José.
Conde del Cascabel, El. In per. REG CULT YUC,
año 2, num. 7, 1944.
Gil González de Avila. In anthol. 12/2768.
Hija del rey, La. (México : UNAM, 1941)
Irene. In per. REG CULT YUC, año 1, num. 4-5,
1943.

Pereña, Alfredo.
Escoba verde, La. (México : Compañía Mexicana Impresora, 1954; 20/4226)

Perés de Arce, Camilo see Ernhard, James.

Pérez Pardella, Agustín.
Siete muertes del general, Las. (Buenos Aires : Ministerio de Educación y Justicia, 1964; 28/2326)

Pérez Taylor, Rafael.
Contrastes de la vida. In coll. 1/2117.
Del hampa. In coll. 1/2117.
Infamia, La. In coll. 1/2117.
Líder, El. In coll. 1/2117.
Lo que devuelve la ciudad. In coll. 1/2117.
Mi hijo! In coll. 1/2117.

Perrín, Tomás.
Foro de México; o, El drama de una comedia. In anthol. 16/2790.

Pico, Pedro E.
Agua en las manos. (Buenos Aires : Argentores, 1951);
also in anthol. 23/5309.
Falta de pan, A. In anthol. 21/4209.
Historia se repita, La. (Buenos Aires : Argentores,
1945)
Napoleoncito. (Madrid : Rivadeneyra, 1933)

Novia de los forasteros, La. In coll. 0/72.

Pueblerina. In coll. 0/72.

Rayas de una cruz, Las. (Buenos Aires : La Argentina, 1940)

Trigo guacho. In anthol. 0/30.

Usted no me gusta, señora! (Buenos Aires : Argentores, 1940)

Verdad en los ojos, La. (Buenos Aires : Argentores, 1934)

Yo no sé decir que no! (Buenos Aires : Argentores, 1934)

Pico, Pedro E. and Bengoa, Juan León.
     Grieta, La. (Buenos Aires : Claridad, 1925)

Pico, Pedro E. and Eichelbaum, Samuel.
     Cáscara de nuez, La. In per. TEAT POP, año 4, num. 133, 1921.
     Doctor. In per. BAMBAL, año 6, num. 254, 1923.

*Piñera, Virgilio.
     Aire frío. (La Habana : Pagrán, 1959; 23/5337); also in coll. 25/4574.
     Boda, La. In coll. 25/4574.
     Electra Garrigó. In coll. 25/4574.
     Falsa alarma. In coll. 25/4574.
     Filántropo, El. In coll. 25/4574.
     Flaco y el gordo, El. In coll. 25/4574.
     Jesús. In coll. 25/4574; also in per. PROMETEO, v. 3, num. 26, jun. '51, p. 26-32 (17/2561)

Pitol, Sergio.
     Regreso, El. In per. UV/PH, 18, abr-jun. '61, p. 301-306 (26/1870)

Piza, José, jt. auth. see under Azevedo, Arthur.

*Plá, Josefina and Centurión Miranda, R.
     Aquí no ha pasado nada. (Asunción : Imp. Nacional, 1945; 11/3340)

Planchart, Julio.
     República de Caín, La. (Caracas : Elite, 1936; 2/2667)

Planchart, María Luisa de.
     Primores de navidad. (Caracas : Fundación Eugenio Mendoza, 1952; 18/2694)

Plaza, Angélica.
    Coyote hambriento. In coll. 20/4227.
    Dioses y lianas. In coll. 20/4227.
    Vencedor del fuego. In coll. 20/4227.

Plaza Noblía, Héctor.
    Cajita de música. In coll. 19/5171.
    Casa quinta, La. (Montevideo, 1953)
    Enfermedad de Arlequín, La. (Montevideo, 1961; 25/
        4575)
    Tarde. In coll. 19/5171.

Podestá, José, jt. auth. see under Gutiérrez, Eduardo.

Pondal Ríos, Sixto.
    Amanecer sobre las ruinas. (Buenos Aires : Claridad,
        1935)

Pondal Ríos, Sixto and Olivari, Carlos A.
    Maridos engañan de 7 a 9, Los. (Buenos Aires :
        Tespis, 1957; 21/4226)

*Ponferrada, Juan Oscar.
    Carnaval del diablo, El. (Buenos Aires : Tespis, 1958;
        22/5325); also in anthol. 23/5309.
    Trigo es de dios, El. (Buenos Aires : Secretaría de
        Cultura, 1947)

*Pongetti, Henrique.
    Society em Baby Doll. In per. RTB, num. 313, j/f
        '60.

Porto, Miguel Antonio.
    En la pasión el martirio. (La Habana : Belascoaín,
        1950; 21/2791)

Potts, Renée.
    Imagíname infinita. In anthol. 0/102.

Prieto, Carlos.
    Jugo de la tierra, El. In anthol. 26/1882.
    Lépero, El. In anthol. 21/4227.

Princivalle, Carlos Maria.
    Caín y Abel. In coll. 0/73.
    Higuerón, El. (Montevideo : García, 1924)
    Hombre de la selva, El. (Montevideo : La Facultad,
        1930)

Juan. (Montevideo : La Facultad, 1945)
Laureles viejos. In per. PEGASO, mar. '22, p. 388-
   402.
Pulgarcito. (Montevideo : La Facultad, 1935)
Toro, El. In coll. 0/73.
Ultimo hijo del sol, El. (Montevideo : García, 1921)
Laureles. In coll. 0/73.
Viajeras en la bruma. In per. UMIP/RN, año 11,
   v. 39, num. 116, ag. '48, p. 208-263 (14/2961)

*Queiroz, Rachel de.
   Beata Maria do Egito, A. (Rio : Olympio, 1958; 21/
      4330)
   Lampião. (Rio : Olympio, 1953; 19/5356)

Ramirez M. , José.
   El, ella y el otro. (México : Sociedad General de
      Autores de México, 1948; 14/2962)

Ramos, José Antonio.
   Tembladera. In anthol. 0/102.

Rapoport, Nicolás.
   Intrusa, La. In coll. 20/4228.
   Manantial, El. In coll. 20/4228.
   Otoñal. In coll. 20/4228.
   Porque soy una mujer. In coll. 20/4228.

Rebêlo, Marques.
   Rua Alegre no. 12. (Curytiba : Ed. Guaira, 1940; 6/
      4408)

*Rechani Agrait, Luis.
   Mi señoria. (San Juan : Puerto Rico Ilustrado, 1940);
      also in anthol. 24/5639.
   Todos los ruiseñores cantan. In anthol. 28/2292.

Rega Molina, Horacio.
   Polifemo; o, Las peras del olmo. (Buenos Aires :
      Poseidon, 1945; 11/3341)
   Posada del León, La. (Buenos Aires : Tor, 1936)
   Vida está lejos, La. (Buenos Aires : Ediciones Con-
      ducta, 1942)

*Reguera Saumell, Manuel.
   Recuerdos de tulipa. In per. UV/PH, 2. época, 27,
      julio-sept. '63, p. 475-510 (28/2327)

Rendón, Victor Manuel.
    Almas hermosas. <u>In</u> coll. 3/3330.
    Ausentismo, El. (<u>Guayaquil : Prensa ecuatoriana,
        1923); <u>also in</u> coll. 3/3330.
    Billete de <u>lotería</u>, El. <u>In</u> coll. 3/3330.
    Carretilla, La. <u>In</u> coll. 3/3330.
    Charito. <u>In</u> coll. 0/74.
    Con victoria y gloria, paz. (Guayaquil : Impr. Guten-
        berg, 1923); <u>also in</u> coll. 3/3330.
    Cuadro heroico. <u>In</u> coll. 3/3330.
    En fuente florida. <u>In</u> coll. 0/74.
    Hoy, ayer y mañana. (Guayaquil : Prensa ecuatoriana,
        1922); <u>also in</u> coll. 3/3330.
    Madrinas de guerra. (Guayquil, 1923); <u>also in</u> coll. 3/
        3330.
    Matrimonio eugénico, El. (Guayaquil : Imp. Gutenberg,
        1923); <u>also in</u> coll. 3/3330.
    Periquín; o, La noche sabrosa. (Guayaquil : J. T.
        Foyain, 1925); <u>also in</u> coll. 3/3330.
    Salus populi. <u>In</u> coll. 0/74.
    Tres victorias, Las. <u>In</u> coll. 3/3330.

*Rengifo, César.
    Lo que dejó la tempestad. <u>In</u> anthol. 28/2388b.

*Requena, María Asunción.
    Ayayema. (Santiago : Sociedad de Escritores de Chile,
        1964; 28/2328)
    Fuerte Bulnes. <u>In</u> per. TEAT. UN. CHILE, num. 5,
        ag. '55, p. 37-79.

*Retes, Ignacio.
    Ciudad para vivir, Una. <u>In</u> anthol. 20/4234.

Reyes, Alfonso.
    Ifigenia cruel. (México : La Cigarra, 1945); <u>also in</u>
        anthol. 20/4234.
    Landrú. <u>In</u> anthol. 28/2301.

*Rial, José Antonio.
    Armadores de la goleta "Ilusión". (Madrid : Oceánida,
        1950)
    Nuramí. (Caracas : Tip. Nación, 1954; 19/5172)

Ríos, Juan.
    Ayar manko. <u>In</u> anthol. 0/12; <u>also in</u> per. MER PER,
        año 29, 35:326, mayo '54, p. 265-308 (20/4229)
    Bufones, Los. <u>In</u> coll. 26/1871.

Desesperados, Los. In coll. 26/1871.
Don Quijote. In coll. 26/1871; also in anthol. 14/2966.
Fuego, El. In coll. 26/1871.
Reino sobre las tumbas, El. In coll. 26/1871.
Selva, La. In coll. 26/1871.

Rivera Alvarez, Edmundo.
Cielo se rindió al amanecer, El. In anthol. 28/2291.

*Robles, J. Humberto.
Desarraigados, Los. (México : INBA, 1962; 26/1872)

Roca Rey, Bernardo.
Muerte de Atahualpa, La. (Lima : Univ. de San Mar-
cos, 1951); also in anthol. 0/12.
Nuevo pueblo ha de nacer, Un. (Lima, 1948)

Rocha, Aurimar.
Elegantes, Os. In per. RTB, num. 327, m/j '62.

Rocha, Daniel, jt. auth. see under Wanderley, José.

Rodrigues, Ferreira.
Bobalhão, O. In per. RTB, num. 254, j/f '50.
Homem que não soube amar, O. (Rio : Sociedade Bra-
sileira de Autores Teatrais, 1944; 10/3916)

*Rodrigues, Nelson.
7 gatinhos, Os. In coll. 25/4729.
Album de família. In coll. 25/4729.
Anjo negro. In coll. 14/3076 and 25/4729.
Beijo no asfalto, O. (Rio : José Ozon, 1961; 26/2078a)
Bôca de ouro. In coll. 25/4729.
Doroteía. In coll. 25/4729.
Falecida, A. In coll. 25/4729.
Mulher sem pecado, A. In coll. 14/3076 and 25/4729.
Perdoa-me por me traíres. In coll. 25/4729.
Senhora dos afogados. In coll. 25/4729.
Valso No. 6. In coll. 25/4729.
Vestido de noiva. In coll. 14/3076 and 25/4729.
Viúva, porém honesta. In coll. 25/4729.

Rodríguez, Franklin.
Ultimo instante, El. In anthol. 28/2388b.

*Rodríguez Galván, Ignacio.
Muñoz, visitador de México. (México : UNAM, 1947;
13/2236)

Rodríguez, Yamandú.
    1810.   (Montevideo : García, 1935; also Paraná, 1950);
        also in anthol. 24/5640.
    Demonio de los Andes, El. In coll. 0/75.
    Fraile Aldao. In coll. 0/75.
    Matrero, El. (Buenos Aires : Perrotti, 1931; also
        Montevideo : Vaglio, 1945)
    Renacentista. In coll. 0/75.

*Roepke, Gabriela.
    Mariposa blanca, Una. In per. UCCH/A, 13, jul '61,
        p. 20-45 (28/2329); also in English as A white
        butterfly in anthol. 0/101.

Rojas, Ricardo.
    Casa colonial, La. In per. NOSOTROS, año 3, num.
        22-23, 1938, p. 3-60, 153-175 (4/3982)
    Elelín. (Buenos Aires : Roldán, 1929)
    Libertad civil, La. (Buenos Aires : Coni, 1924)
    Ollántay. (Buenos Aires : Losada, 1939; 7/3773); also
        in anthol. 20/4201.
    Salamanca, La. (Buenos Aires : Losada, 1943)

Romero de Terreros y Vinent, Manuel.
    Casa de huéspedes. In coll. 21/4228.
    Confesión, La. In coll. 21/4228.
    Intuición. In coll. 21/4228.
    Juez, El. In coll. 21/4228.
    Luciferina. In coll. 21/4228.
    Paso macabro. In coll. 21/4228.

Romero Peláez, Celso.
    Drama de Bolivar, El.   (Bogotá : Editorial Centro,
        1942)
    Lincoln, el leñador.   (Santiago : Tegualda, 1948; 14/
        2963)

*Rosencof, Mauricio.
    Ranas, Las. (Montevideo : Ediciones Siglo Ilustrado,
        1961; 26/1873)

Rosenrauch, E.
    Cristo en el desierto. In coll. 21/4229.
    Reo en capilla. In coll. 21/4229.
    Tambores, Los. In coll. 21/4229.

Rubertino, María Luisa.
    Cerco, El. (Buenos Aires : Tespis, 1957; 21/4230)

Silencio, El.   (Buenos Aires : Americalee, 1946)

Ruiz Aldea, Pedro.
    Provincianos de 1862, Los.   In anthol. 18/2698.

Ruiz, Raúl.
    Niño que quiere hacer las tareas, El.   In per.   UCCH/
        A, 14, ag. '61, p. 16-32 (28/2330)

Sábat Ercasty, Carlos.
    Demonio de Don Juan, El.   (Montevideo : García, 1934;
        1/2118)
    Prometeo.   (Santiago, 1952)

Sábato, Ernesto.
    Vieja bandera, La.   In per.   F, 21, sep-oct. '59, p. 42-
        51 (24/5629)

Sabido, Miguel.
    Romanza, La.   In per.   UV/PH, 22, abr.-jun. '62,
        p. 255-268 (26/1874)

Sada Hermosillo, Concepción.
    Hora del festin, La.   (México : Plycsa, 1937)
    Mundo para mí, Un.   In anthol. 20/4234.
    Tercer personaje, El.   (México : Sociedad General de
        Autores de México, 1949; 15/2443)

*Sáenz, Dalmiro.
    Qwertyuiop.   (Buenos Aires : Goyanarte, 1961; 26/1875)

*Salazar Bondy, Sebastián.
    Algo que quiere morir.   (Buenos Aires : Talía, 1956;
        24/5630); also in coll. 26/1876.
    Amore, gran laberinto.   In anthol. 14/2966.
    El de la valija.   (Lima, 1954)
    Fabricante de deudas, El.   In anthol. 28/2388b.
    Flora tristán.   In coll. 26/1876.
    No hay isla feliz.   (Lima : Ediciones Club de Teatro,
        1954; 20/4230); also in coll. 26/1876; also in an-
        thol. 0/12.
    Novios, Los.   In per.   MORADAS, v. 2, num. 6,
        oct. '48, p. 225-233 (14/2964)
    Rabdomante, El.   In per.   CDLA, 5:31, jul-ag. '65,
        p. 71-81 (28/2331)
    Rodil, El.   (Lima : Tip. Peruana, 1952); also in coll.
        26/1876.

Salazar Bondy, Sebastián, jt. auth. see under Miró, César.

Saldías, José Antonio.
    Candidato del pueblo, El. In anthol. 21/4209.
    Gomina y jazz-band. (Buenos Aires : L. J. Rosso,
        1928)
    Gringa Federika, La. (Buenos Aires : Argentores,
        1940)

Salgado, Antoine.
    Rivière rouge, La. (Port-au-Prince : Imp. La Gazette
        du Palais, 1953; 20/4459)

Salinas, Marcelo.
    Alma guajira. In anthol. 0/102.

Salinas Pérez, Pablo.
    Gigante y el enano, El. In coll. 24/5632.
    Hombrecillos de gris, Los. In coll. 24/5632.
    Madre y el muro, La. In coll. 24/5632.

*Sampaio, José da Silveira.
    Deu Freud contra. (Rio : Talmagráfica, 1954)
    Triângulo escaleno. In per. TEAT BR, 6, abr. '56,
        p. 21-27 (20/4422)

Sampaio, José da Silveira and Faro, Arnaldo.
    Futebol em família. In per. RTB, num. 282, n/d
        '54.

Sampaio, Moreira, jt. auth. see under Azevedo, Arthur.

*Sánchez, Florencio.
    Barranca abajo. In coll. 0/10, 0/76, 0/77, 0/82,
        0/83, 0/84, 0/87, 17/2562, 18/2695; also in
        anthol. 22/5315, 24/5626, and 24/5640; also in
        French as Tout s'écroule in coll. 0/86.
    Buen negocio, Un. In coll. 0/10, 0/87, 17/2562, and
        18/2695.
    Canillita. In coll. 0/78, 0/85, 0/87, 17/2562, and
        18/2695.
    Cedulas de San Juan. In coll. 0/10, 0/78, 0/87, 17/
        2562, and 18/2695.
    Curdas, Los. In coll. 0/85, 0/87, 17/2562, and 18/
        2695.
    Derechos de la salud, Los. In coll. 0/10, 0/79, 0/81,
        0/83, 0/87, 17/2562, and 18/2695; also in anthol.
        20/4201.

Desalojo, El. In coll. 0/10, 0/76, 0/81, 0/83, 0/87, 17/2562, and 18/2695.

En familia. In coll. 0/10, 0/79, 0/81, 0/83, 0/87, 17/2562, and 18/2695; also in French as En famille in coll. 0/86.

Gente honesta, La. In coll. 0/87, 17/2562, and 18/2695.

Gringa, La. (New York : Knopf, 1927; also Crofts, 1938); also in coll. 0/10, 0/76, 0/82, 0/83, 0/84, 0/87, 17/2562, and 18/2695; also in English as The foreign girl; Stanford U., 1942; and in anthol. 0/80.

Mano santa. In coll. 0/85, 0/87, 17/1562, and 18/2695.

Marta Gruni. In coll. 0/84, 0/87, 17/2562, and 18/2695.

M'hijo el dotor. (Buenos Aires : Kapelusz, 1953); also in coll. 0/10, 0/81, 0/83, 0/87, 17/2562, and 18/2695; also in French as Mon fils le docteur in coll. 0/86.

Moneda falsa. (Buenos Aires : Quetzal, 1953); also in coll. 0/10, 0/79, 0/81, 0/83, 0/87, 17/2562, and 18/2695; also in French as Fausse monnaie in coll. 0/86.

Muertos, Los. (Buenos Aires : Argentores, 1935); also in coll. 0/77, 0/82, 0/83, 0/85, 0/87, 17/2562, and 18/2695; also in French as Les morts in coll. 0/86.

Nuestros hijos. In coll. 0/10, 0/82, 0/83, 0/87, 17/2562, and 18/2695.

Pasado, El. In coll. 0/10, 0/87, 17/2562, and 18/2695.

Pobre gente, La. In coll. 0/10, 0/87, 17/2562, and 18/2695.

Puertas adentro. In coll. 0/87, 17/2562, and 18/2695.

Tigra, La. In coll. 0/87, 17/2562, and 18/2695.

Sánchez Galarraga, Gustavo.
Buen camino, El. In coll. 0/88.
Carmen. In coll. 0/88.
Compuesta, y sin novio. In coll. 0/88.
Conferencia contra el hombre. In coll. 0/88.
Dos de mayo. In coll. 0/88.
Filibustero, El. In coll. 0/88.
Héroe, El. (New York : Oxford UP, 1941; 7/4710); also in coll. 0/88.
Mundo de los muñecos, El. In coll. 0/88.
Princesa buena, La. In coll. 0/88.

Sangre mambisa. In coll. 0/88.
Ultima corrida, La. In coll. 0/88.
Ultimo areito, El. In coll. 0/88.

Sánchez Gardel, Julio.
Campanas, Las. In coll. 20/4231.
Mirasoles, Los. (Buenos Aires : Pan América, 1939);
also in coll. 20/4231.
Montaña de las brujas, La. In coll. 20/4231; also in
English as The witches' mountain in anthol. 0/89.
Noche de luna. In coll. 20/4231.

*Sánchez, Luis Rafael.
Angeles se han fatigado, Los. In coll. 25/4576; also
in anthol. 26/1883.
Farsa del amor compadrito. In coll. 25/4576.
Hiel nuestra de cada día, La. In anthol. 26/1883.
O casi el alma. In anthol. 28/2292.

Sánchez Maldonado, Benjamín.
Herencia de Canuto, La. In anthol. 26/1880.
Hijos de Thalía, Los; o, Bufos de fin de siglo. In an-
thol. 26/1880.

*Sánchez Mayans, Fernando.
Alas del pez, Las. In per. INDA/CBA, 1:3, oct. '60,
p. 41-92 (25/4577)
Joven drama. In anthol. 28/2301.

Sánchez Varona, Ramón.
Amor perfecto, El. (La Habana : Selecta, 1948; 14/
2965)
Sombra, La. (La Habana : Alfa, 1938)

Sancho, Alfredo.
Alcmeónides, Los. (San Salvador : Ministerio de Edu-
cación, 1961; 25/4578)
Débora. (San José : Impr. Nacional, 1955)

*Sándor, Malena.
Tu vida y la mía. (Buenos Aires : Argentores, 1945)
Y la respuesta fue dada. (Buenos Aires : Tespis,
1957; 23/5339)

Santander, Felipe.
Luna de miel ... para diez. In anthol. 26/1882.

Santibañes, César de.
  Omnibus 58.   (La Plata : Municipalidad de La Plata,
      1962; 26/1877)

Santos, Justino.
  Raios Y, Os. In per. RTB, num. 314, m/a '60.

Santos, Miguel.
  Banquete do prefeito. In per. RTB, num. 297, m/j
      '57.
  Hotel dos amores. In per. RTB, num. 269, s/o '52.
  Não posso viver assim! In per. RTB, num. 320, m/
      a '61.
  Visita de cerimônia, Uma. In per. RTB, num. 295,
      j/f '57.

Santos, Miguel and Iglezias, Luiz.
  Priminho do coração. In per. RTB, num. 264, n/d
      '51.

Santos, Miguel, jt. auth. see under Boscoli, Geysa.

Saráh Comandari, Roberto.
  Algún día ... (Santiago, 1950; 16/2793)

Sarobe, Angélica.
  Selva y petróleo. (Buenos Aires : Tespis, 1957; 23/
      5340)

Schaefer Gallo, Carlos.
  Ciudad roja, La. (Milano : G. Ricordi, 1938)
  Raíz en la piedra, La. (Buenos Aires : Tespis, 1960;
      25/4579)

Schroeder Inclán, Federico.
  Hidalgo. (México : Editorial Intercontinental, 1953)
  Hoy invita la güera. In anthol. 20/4234.

Segovia, Tomás.
  Zamora bajo los astros.   (México : Impr. Universitaria,
      1959; 23/5341)

*Segura, Manuel Ascensio.
  Moza mala, La. In coll. 24/5633.
  Na catita. In coll. 0/90; also in anthol. 20/4201.
  Pepa, La. In per. B INST RIVA AGÜERO, 1:1, 1951-
      52, p. 117-195 (18/2696)

Sargente Canuto, El. In coll. 0/90 and 24/5633; also
    in anthol. 22/5315.
Saya y manto, La. In coll. 0/90.

Seljan, Zora.
    Festa do Bomfim, A. (Rio : Livraria São José, 1958;
        23/5555)
    Iansan - mulher de Xangô. In coll. 22/5528.
    Orelha de Obâ, A. In coll. 22/5528.
    Oxum abalô. In coll. 22/5528.

Seoane, Luis.
    Soldadera, La. (Buenos Aires : Ariadna, 1957; 21/
        4231)

Sepúlveda Iriondo, Ariel.
    Fernando Morales. (Rosario : Imprenta de Revista Mod-
        erna, 1953; 19/5173)

Sierra Berdecía, Fernando.
    Esta noche juega el jóker. (San Juan : Biblioteca de
        Autores Puertorriqueños, 1939; 2nd ed. 1948; 21/
        4232); also in anthol. 24/5639.

Sierra, Justo.
    Piedad. In coll. 15/2444.

*Sieveking, Alejandro.
    Madre de los conejos, La. In per. ESCENA, 1:1,
        abr. '61, p. 1-25 (26/1878)

Silberstein, Enrique.
    Necesito diez mil pesos. In anthol. 26/1863.

Silva, Antônio José da.
    Amphytrião ou Jupiter e Alcmena. In coll. 6/4410.
    Guerras do Alecrim e da Mangerona. In coll. 6/4410,
        22/5529.
    Vida de Esopo, A. In coll. 22/5529.

Silva Gutiérrez, Jaime.
    Otro avaro, El. (Santiago : Ediciones del Joven Lau-
        rel, 1954; 20/4232)

Silva Valdés, Fernán.
    Barrio Palermo. (Montevideo, 1953); also in coll. 22/
        5327.
    Burlador de la pampa, El. In anthol. 24/5640.

Por la gracia de Dios. (Montevideo : Revista Nacional, 1954); also in coll. 22/5327.

Santos Vega. (Montevideo : A. Monteverde, 1952; 18/2697); also in coll. 22/5327.

Silvain, Julio César.
Heladera, La. In coll. 28/2332.
Oportunidad, La. In coll. 28/2332.
Pilar, El. In coll. 28/2332.

Silveira, Helena.
No fundo do poço. (São Paulo : Martins, 1950; 16/2918)

Soferman, Arturo.
Enanito feo, El. (Montevideo : Editorial Galería Libertad; 26/1879)

*Solana, Rafael.
A su imagen y semejanza. In coll. 24/5635.
Bomba atómica, La. (México : A. R. Vicario, 1946)
Casa de la santísima, La. (México : Ediciones Oasis, 1960; 24/5634)
Debiera haber obispas. In anthol. 20/4234.
Ensalada de noche buena. In anthol. 28/2306.
Espada en mano. In coll. 24/5635.
Estrella que se apaga. (México : Editorial Intercontinental, 1953; 19/5174)
Ilustre cuna, La. In per. PANOR TEAT MEX, 1:6, en. '55, p. 19-46 (20/4233)
Isla de oro, La. (México, 1954)
Ni lo mande Dior. (México : Editorial Intercontinental, 1958; 22/5328); also in anthol. 23/5348.
Sólo quedaban las plumas. (México : Ecuador, 1961; 25/4580)

*Solari Swayne, Enrique.
Campana y la fuente, La. (Lima : Historia, 1945)
Collacocha. (Lima : Populibros Peruanos, 1955; also 1963; 28/2333); also in anthol. 0/12.

Solly.
Crack, El. (Buenos Aires : Nueva América, 1960; 24/5636)

*Solórzano, Carlos.
Cruce de vías. In coll. 23/5342.

Crucificado, El. In coll. 23/5342; also in anthol. 21/
4227.

Doña Beatriz, la sin ventura. (México : Helio-Mexico,
1954; 19/5175); also in per. CAM, v. 59, sep.-
oct. '51, p. 215-266 (17/2563).

Hechicero, El. (México : Cuad. Americanos, 1955;
19/5176)

Manos de Dios, Las. (México : Costa-Amic, 1937;
also 1957; 21/4233); also in anthol. 28/2388b.

Sueño del ángel, El. In anthol. 24/5644.

Sotoconil, Rubén.
Chicharra y las hormigas, La. In anthol. 22/5329.

Sousa, Afonso Felix de.
Caminho de Belém. (Rio : Livros de Portugal, 1962;
28/2658)

*Souto, Alexandrino de.
Menina que vendia flores, A. In per. RTB, num. 311,
s/o '59.

Souza, Antonio.
Pascuatina. In per. PAU/AM, v. 9, dec. '57.

Spota, Luis.
Aria de los sometidos, El. (México : B. Costa-Amic,
1962; 25/4581)
Dos veces la lluvia. In coll. 0/91.
Ellos pueden esperar. In coll. 0/91.

*Steiner, Rolando.
Judit. In anthol. 23/5346.

*Suassuna, Ariano.
Auto da compadecida. (Rio : Agir, 1957; 21/4331); also
in anthol. 28/2654. Also in English as Rogues'
trial (Berkeley : University of California Press,
1963; 26/2079)

Subercaseaux, Benjamín.
Cháina-boy. (Santiago : Imp. Universitaria, 1938; 4/
3983)
Pasión y epopeya de Halcón Ligero. (Santiago : Nascimento, 1957; 22/5330)

Tabárez, Américo see Correa, Pancho.

*Tálice, Roberto Alejandro.
Gran farsa, La. (Montevideo : J. Serrano, 1922)

Tálice, Roberto Alejandro and De Stefani, Alejandro.
Sábado del pecado. (Buenos Aires : Tespis, 1961; 24 /
5637)

Tálice, Roberto Alejandro and Montaine, Eliseo.
Noche en los ojos. (Buenos Aires : Argentores, 1947)

Tarruella, Víctor.
Brasas, Las. In per. CCE/R, 10:19, jul-dic. '57,
p. 282-288 (22/5331)

Terbay, Andrés see Saráh Comandari, Roberto.

Testena, Folco, jt. auth. see under García Velloso, Enrique.

*Thomas, José de.
Isla interior. (Buenos Aires : Cooperativa Impresora
y Dist. Argentina, 1959; 23/5345)
Televisor, El. (Buenos Aires : Talía, 1962; 26/1884)

Tigre, Manoel Bastos.
Cabelo branco, O. In per. RTB, num. 223, j/a/s
'44.
Micróbio do amor, O. In per. RTB, num. 316, j/a
'60.

Tinoco, Godofredo.
Judas no tribunal. In per. RTB, num. 321, m/j '61.

*Tojeiro, Gastão.
A tal que entrou no escuro; ou, A bondosa Gelásia Kent.
(Rio : Simões, 1952)
"As" do volante, O. (Rio : Coelho, 1941)
Cazuza arranjou outra, O. (Rio : Coelho, 1941)
"Fans" de Robert Taylor, As: ou, Um galã que não faz
fitas. (Rio : Sociedade Brasileira de Autores Tea-
trais, 1940)
Felisberto do café, O; ou, A conferencia do garçon.
(Rio : Coelho, 1941)
Filho do Rei do Prégo, O. In per. RTB, num. 250,
m/a '49.
Inquilina de Botafogo, A; ou, As inquilinas do Desiderio.
(Rio : Sociedade Brasileira de Autores Teatrais,
1933)

Minha sogra é da polícia, ou A rival de Sherlock
    Holmes. (Rio : Simões, 1952; 18/2818)
Onde canta o sabiá. (Rio : Coelho, 1931); also in per.
    RTB, num. 255, m/a '50.
Sai da porta, Deolinda! ou, Um sobrinho igual ao tio.
    (Rio : Coelho, 1943; 9/4299)
Se não fosse o telefone. (Rio : Coelho, 1943)
Simpatico Jeremias, O. (Rio : Flores & Mano, 1935)
Solteira é que não fico. (Rio : Coelho, 1943)
Sonhos de Teodoro. (Rio : Editôra Talmagráfica, 1951)
"Tenente" era o porteiro, O. (Rio : Sociedade Brasil-
    eria de Autores Teatrais, 1938)
Vasco ganha sempre, O. (Rio : Sociedade Brasileira
    de Autores Teatrais, 1954)
Vendedora de recursos, Uma. (Rio : Coelho, 1943)

Torres Chaves, Efraín.
    Crimen del silencio, El. (Quito : Tall. Graf. Nacion-
        ales, 1948)
    Pirámides truncadas. (Quito : Editôra Quito, 194?)
    Trayectoria de los semi-locos, La. (Quito : Editorial
        Fray Jodoco Ricke, 1952; 18/2699)

*Tourinho, Nazareno.
    Nó de várias pernas ou nó de 4 pernas. (Belém :
        Gráfica Falangola Editôra, 1961; 25/4730)

Trejo, Mario and Vanasco, Alberto.
    No hay piedad para Hamlet (Buenos Aires : Ministerio
        de Educación y Justicia, 1960; 25/4583)

*Trejo, Nemesio.
    Devotos, Los. In anthol. 21/4209.
    Mujeres lindas, Las. (Buenos Aires : Bambalinas,
        1922)
    Políticos, Los. In anthol. 24/5627.

*Triana, José.
    Mayor general, El. In coll. 26/1885.
    Medea en el espejo. In coll. 26/1885.
    Muerte del ñeque, La. (La Habana : Ediciones Revolu-
        ción, 1964; 28/2336)
    Noche de los asesinos, La. (La Habana : Casa de las
        Américas, 1965; 28/2337)
    Parque de la fraternidad. In coll. 26/1885.

Trovão da Costa, Maria Jacintha.
    Conflito. (Pôrto Alegre : Meridiano, 1942)

Trovão de Campos, Maria Jacinta.
    Gosto da vida, O.   (Rio, 1940; 5/3991)

Uhthoff, Enrique.
    Amar, eso es todo.   (México : Sociedad General de
        Autores de México, 1949; 15/2445)

Urueta de Villaseñor, Margarita   see Urueta, Margarita.

Urueta, Margarita.
    Ave de sacrificio.   (México : Letras de México, 1945;
    Mansión para turistas.   In coll. 0/92.
    San Lunes.   In 0/92.
    Una hora de vida.   In coll. 0/92.

*Usigli, Rodolfo.
    4 Chemins 4.   In coll. 28/2339.
    Aguas estancadas.   In coll. 28/2339.
    Alcestes.   In coll. 28/2339.
    Apóstol, El.   In coll. 28/2339.
    Corona de luz: la Virgen.   (México : Fondo de Cultura
        Económica, 1965; 28/2338)
    Corona de sombra.   (México : Cuadernos Americanos,
        1947; 13/2237; also 1958; 22/5332; also New York :
        Appleton-Century-Crofts, 1961; 24/5641); also in
        anthol. 22/5315; also in English as Crown of
        shadows (London : Wingate, 1946)
    Crítica de "la mujer no hace milagros".   In coll. 28/2339.
    Estado de secreto.   In coll. 28/2339.
    Exposición, La.   In CAM, 53, 1960 (24/5642)
    Falso drama.   In coll. 28/2339.
    Familia cena en casa, La.   (México : Sociedad General
        de Autores de México, 1942); also in per.   HIJO
        PRODIGO, año 2, v. 6, num. 21, dic. '44, p. 165-
        183; v. 7, num. 22, en. '45, p. 42-56; num. 23,
        feb. '45, p. 109-120 (11/3343)
    Función de despedida, La.   (México : Editorial Inter-
        continental, 1952; 18/2700)
    Gesticulador, El.   (México : Letras de México, 1947;
        10/3680); also in coll. 28/2339; also in anthol. 20/
        4234 and 24/5638.
    Jano es una muchacha.   (México, 1952)
    Medio tono.   (México : Editorial Dialéctica, 1938; 4/
        3984); also in coll. 28/2339.
    Mientras amemos.   (México, 1948); also in coll. 28/
        2339; also in per.   PAN, 1, primavera '56 (20/
        4235)

Mujer no hace milagros, La. (México : Secretaria de Educación Pública, 1949; 15/2446); also in coll. 28/2339.

Niño y la niebla, El. (México : Nuevo Mundo, 1951; 17/2564); also in coll. 28/2339.

Noche del estío. In coll. 28/2339.

Otra primavera. (México : Sociedad General de Autores de México, 1947; 13/2238; also 1956; 22/5333); also in coll. 28/2339.

Presidente y el ideal, El. In coll. 28/2339.

Sueño de día. (México : América, 1949)

Tres comedias impolíticas. In coll. 28/2339.

Ultima puerta, La. In coll. 28/2339.

Vacaciones. (México : Secretaria de Educación Pública, 1948); also in anthol. 24/5644.

Uslar-Pietri, Arturo.
Chúo Gil y las tejedoras. (Caracas : Tip. Vargas, 1960; 23/5347)
Día de Antero Albán, El. In coll. 22/5334.
Dios invisible, El. In coll. 22/5334.
Fuga de Miranda. In coll. 22/5334.
Tebaida, La. In coll. 22/5334.

*Vacarezza, Alberto.
Baile en la bateria, Un. In per. ESCENA, año 14, num. 673, 1931.
Broma pesada. In coll. 0/93.
Cabo Rivero, El. In per. ESCENA, año 11, num. 514, 1928.
Cambaleche de la buena suerte, El. In per. ESCENA, año 8, num. 343, 1925.
Camino a la tablada, El. In per. ESCENA, año 13, num. 643, 1930.
Casa de los Batallán, La. (Buenos Aires : Argentores, 1940)
Chacarita. In per. ESCENA, año 7, num. 330, 1924.
Conventillo de la paloma, El. In per. ESCENA, año 12, num. 585, 1929.
Conventillo del gavilán, El. In per. ESCENA, año 14, num. 682, 1931.
Conventillo nacional. In per. ESCENA, año 8, num. 379, 1925.
Escrushantes, Los. In anthol. 24/5627.
Fondén de la alegría, El. In per. ESCENA, año 14, num. 668, 1931.
Minas de Caminiaga, Las. (Buenos Aires : Argentores, 1936)

Otra noche en los corrales, La. In per. ESCENA,
    año 13, num. 602, 1930.
Paco mocho, El. In coll. 0/93.
Paso cambiado. In coll. 0/93.
Prosa y verso. In coll. 0/93.
Registro civil. In coll. 0/93.
San Antonio de los Cobres. (Buenos Aires : Argentores,
    1940)
Sota en puerta, La. In coll. 0/93.
Sunchales. In per. ESCENA, año 13, num. 639, 1930.
Teniente peñaloza, El. In per. ESCENA, año 12,
    num. 565, 1930.
Tía Mercedes. In coll. 0/93.
Todo el año es carnaval. In per, ESCENA, año 8,
    num. 348, 1925.
Tu cuna fue un conventillo. In anthol. 21/4209.
Va... cayendo gente al baile! In per. ESCENA, año
    13, num. 609, 1930.
Verbena criolla. In per. ESCENA, año 4, supl. 37,
    1921.
Vida es un sainete, La. In per. ESCENA, año 13,
    num. 354, 1925.

Valencia, Gerardo.
    Chonta. In per. REV INDIAS, v. 31, num. 97, jun.
        '45, suppl. 1, p. 1-41 (13/2239)
    Hada imprecisa, El. In per. UNIV NAC COL, num.
        7, jul-sep. '45, p. 102-124 (12/2767)

Vanasco, Alberto, jt. auth. see under Trejo, Mario.

Vanicóre, Clóris.
    Anfora. (Rio : Irmãos Pongetti Editores, 1964; 28/
        2659)
    Divani. (Rio : Irmãos Pongetti Editores, 1964; 28/
        2660)

Vargas Tejada, Luis.
    Convulsiones, Las. In coll. 0/94; also in English as
        My poor nerves in anthol. 0/80.
    Doraminta. In coll. 0/94.

Velarde, Héctor.
    Hombre con tongo, Un. In per. MAR DEL SUR, año
        1, v. 1, num. 2, n/d '48, p. 41-68 (14/2967)

Vera, Pedro Jorge.
    Ardientes caminos, Los. In coll. 21/4234.

Dios de la selva. In coll. 21/4234.
Mano de Dios, La. In coll. 21/4234.

*Vianna Filho, Oduvaldo.
Chapetuba Futebol Clube. In per. RTB, num. 311,
s/o '59.

*Vianna, Oduvaldo.
Manhãs de sol. In per. RTB, num. 319, j/f '61.

Vianna, Renato.
Deus. In coll. 20/4423.
Divino perfume, O. (Rio : Sociedade Brasileira de
Autores Teatrais, 1932); also in per. RTB, num.
263.
Sexo. In coll. 20/4423.

*Vilalta, Maruxa.
Ultima letra, La. In per. AVANT, num. 314, jul
'64.

*Villaurrutia, Xavier.
Ausente, El. (México : Tierra Nueva, 1942); also in
coll. 9/3950 and 19/5177; also in per. TIERRA
NUEVA, año 3, num. 13-14, jan-apr '42, p. 35-50.
En qué piensas? In coll. 9/3950; also in anthol. 24/
5638; also in per. LET MEX, num. 24, 1938, p.
5-9 (4/3985)
Ha llegado el momento. In coll. 9/3950.
Hiedra, La. (México : Editorial Cultura, 1941); also
in coll. 19/5177.
Invitación a la muerte. (México : Letras de México,
1944; 10/3681; also Sociedad General de Autores
de México, 1948); also in coll. 19/5177.
Juego peligroso. In coll. 19/5177.
Mujer legítima, La. (México : Ed. R. Loera y Chávez,
1943; 9/3951); also in coll. 19/5177.
Mulata de Córdoba, La. (México : Hijo Pródigo, 1945);
also in per. HIJO PRODIGO, año 2, v. 7, num.
24, mar '44, p. 166-183 (11/3344).
Parece mentira. (México : Imprenta Mundial, 1934);
also in coll. 9/3950; also in anthol. 24/5638.
Pobre Barba Azul, El. (México : Sociedad General de
Autores de México, 1947; 13/2240); also in coll.
19/5177.
Sea usted breve. (México : E. Nandino, 1938); also in
coll. 9/3950 and 19/5177; also in anthol. 24/5638.

Solterón, El. (México : Helio-México, 1954; 19/5178);
    also in anthol. 24/5643; also in per. REV GUAT,
    año 1, v. 1, jul-sep. '45, p. 114-129 (11/3345)
Tragedia de las equivocaciones, La. (México : Gráficos
    Guanajuato, 1950; 16/2794); also in coll. 19/5177.
Yerro candente, El. (México : Letras de México, 1945;
    11/3346); also in coll. 19/5177; also in anthol. 20/
    4234.

Villegas Vidal, Juan Carlos.
    Llamado, El. (La Plata : Municipalidad de La Plata,
        1962; 26/1886)

Vitor, Léo.
    Idiota, O. In per. RTB, num. 276, n/d '53.
    Maquina da felicidade, A. In per. RTB, num. 268,
        j/a '52.

*Vodánovic, Sergio.
    Deja que los perros ladren. (Santiago : Editorial del
        Nuevo Extremo, 1960; 24/5645)

Wainer, Alberto.
    Hombre y el bosque, El. In coll. 25/4584.
    Romeo y Julieta. In coll. 25/4584.
    Ultimos, Los. In coll. 25/4584.

*Wanderley, José.
    Compra-se um marido. In per. RTB, num. 257,
        supl. 1950.
    Era uma vez um vagabundo. (Rio : Sociedade Brasil-
        eira de Autores Teatrais, 1940)
    Pertinho do céu. (Rio : Coelho, 1942)
    Uma vez na vida. (Rio : Sociedade Brasileira de Au-
        tores Teatrais, 1952; 18/2819)
    Vida brigou comigo, A. (Rio : Coelho, 1943)

Wanderley, José and Lago, Mario
    Beijo que era meu, "canario. " (Rio : Pedro Primeiro,
        1943)
    Como você quizer. In per. RTB, num. 270, n/d '52.
    Tudo por você. In per. RTB, num. 242, dez. '47.

Wanderley, José and Rocha, Daniel.
    Amo todas as mulheres. (Rio : Sociedade Brasileira
        de Autores Teatrais, 1943)
    Casca grossa, O. In per. RTB, num. 236, jun. '47.

Maluco da família, O. In per. RTB, num. 323, s/o
'61 (28/2661)

Wanderley Menezes, Maria.
Amor na terra do cangaço, O. In per. RTB, num.
330, n/d '62.

Weisbach.
Guaso, El. In anthol. 24/5626.

Wiesse, María.
Extranjera, La. In per. HORA, año 4, num. 43-48,
feb-julio '46, p. 7-20 (13/2241)

*Wolff, Egon.
Invasores, Los. In anthol. 28/2388b.

Wolodarsky, Solly see Solly.

X.
Don Centén. In anthol. 26/1880.

Young, Juan Raul.
Viaje a la costa. (Buenos Aires : Talía, 1963; 26/1887)

Yunque, Alvaro.
13. 313. In coll. 18/2701.
Cinco muchachos. In coll. 0/97.
Diamante en el apéndice, Un. In coll. 18/2701.
Dos humoristas y ella. In coll. 18/2701.
Hijo de la Paula, El. In coll. 0/97.
Libertadores, Los. In coll. 0/97.
Miquel cantó. In coll. 0/96.
Perro atorrante, El. In coll. 0/97.
Somos hermanos. In coll. 0/96 and 0/97.
Tres poetas y un pan. In coll. 0/97.
Vestido nuevo, El. In coll. 0/97.

Zavalía, Alberto de.
Doncella prodigiosa, La. (Buenos Aires : Emecé, 1961;
26/1888)
Octavo día, El. (Buenos Aires : Editorial Sur, 1961;
26/1889)

Zavattini, Cesare and García Berlanga, Luis.
Soldado y criada. In per. N, 6:27, dic. '55, p. 160-
175 (20/4236)

Zendejas, Francisco.
    Jerónimo! (México : Costa-Amic, 1956; 21/4235)

Plays by unknown authors

Amor de la estanciera, El. In anthol. 21/4209 and 22/5312.
Bodas de Chivico y Pancha, Las. In anthol. 22/5312.
Detalle de la Acción de Maipú, El. In anthol. 22/5312.
Entremés de la vieja y el viejo. MAR DEL SUR, v. 2, num.
    5, m/j '49, p. 28-35 (15/2181)
Güegüense, El. In anthol. 12/2765.
Historia de Sansón. In anthol. 12/2765.
Original del jigante. In anthol. 12/2765.
Original de pastores para obsequio del niño Dios. In anthol.
    12/2765.
Pastores, Los. (San Antonio : Treviño Bros. , 1949; 15/
    2442)
Restauración del sacramento, La. In anthol. 12/2765.

Title Index

Fugir, casar ou morrer --
   Magalhães Júnior
Fumadas -- Buttaro
Función de despedida, La --
   Usigli
Función homenaje -- Ferrer
Fundación del desengaño --
   Betti
Funeral home -- Béneke
Futebol em família -- Sampaio,
   José da Silveira
Gabino el mayoral -- García
   Velloso
Gaitana, La -- Díaz Díaz
Gaivota, A -- Fernandes,
   Millôr
Gajo de enebro, El -- Mallea
Galán -- Díaz Díaz
Fallina de los huevos de oro,
   La -- Feder
Gato y su selva, El -- Eichel-
   baum
General Piar, El -- Lasser
Genro de muitas sogras --
   Azevedo, Arthur
Gente honesta, La -- Sánchez,
   Florencio
Gesticulador, El -- Usigli
Gigana me enganou, A -- Mag-
   alhães, Paulo de
Gigante y el enano, El -- Sal-
   inas Pérez
Gigoló -- García Velloso
Gil González de Avila -- Peón
   y Contreras
Gimba, Presidente dos Valentes
   -- Guarnieri
Glaciar, El -- Carballido
Gloria -- González
Gomina y jazz-band -- Saldías
Gorgona, La -- Bourbakis
Gosto da vida, O -- Trovão de
   Campos
Gran farsa, La -- Talice
Grande estiagem, A -- Gondim
Grande remedio -- Camargo,
   Joracy
Gran-fina -- Mesquita

Granfinos em apuros --
   Magalhães, Heloisa
   Helena
Granja -- Montalvo
Grieta, La -- Pico
Gringa, La -- Sánchez,
   Florencio
Gringa Federika, La --
   Saldias
Guapo del 900, Un -- Eich-
   elbaum
Guardia del auxiliar, La --
   Pacheco
Guaso, El -- Weisbach
Güegüense, El -- Author
   unknown
Guerra de las gordas, La
   -- Novo
Guerras do Alecrim e da
   Mangerona -- Silva
Ha llegado el momento --
   Villaurrutia
Ha pasado una mujer --
   Aquino
Há sempre um amanhã --
   Carvalho, Fernando
   Livino de
Ha vuelto Ulises -- Novo
Hacia la meta -- Parada
   Léon
Hacienda de los cuatro --
   Belaval
Hada imprecisa, El --
   Valencia
He visto a Dios -- Defilippis
   Novoa
Hebra de oro, La -- Car-
   ballido
Hechicero, El -- Solórzano
Heladera, La -- Silvain
Helena fechou a porta --
   Accioly Netto
Herencia de águeda, La --
   Feder
Herencia de Canuto, La --
   Sánchez Maldonando
Herencia maldita, La --
   Macau

List of Collections and Anthologies

[Omitted numbers were originally assigned to collections out of the scope of this volume.]

0/1   Feder, Carlos Eduardo. <u>Teatro para leer: la esperanza del mar</u>.... (Buenos Aires : López, 1952)

0/2   Feder, Carlos Eduardo. <u>Teatro para leer: la juventud del cedro</u>.... (Montevideo : Editorial Florensa y Lafón, 1952)

0/3   Feder, Carlos Eduardo. <u>Teatro para leer: Sueño de una tarde de invierno</u>.... (Montevideo : Editorial Florensa y Lafón, 1952)

0/4   Kelly, Celso. <u>Conflitos sentimentias</u>. (Rio : Irmãos Pongetti, 1953)

0/5   Laferrère, Gregorio de. <u>Obras escogidas</u>. (Buenos Aires : Angel Estrada, 1943)

0/7   Machado de Assis, Joaquim Maria. <u>Obras completas: vol. 28, Theatro</u>. (Rio : W. M. Jackson, Inc. , 1937)

0/10   Sánchez, Florencio. <u>Teatro de Florencio Sánchez</u>. (Buenos Aires : Sopena, 1957)

0/11   <u>Los linares</u>. (Buenos Aires : Talía, 1960)

0/12   <u>Teatro peruano contemporaneo</u>. Prol. de José Hesse. (Madrid : Aguilar, 1959)

0/13   Acevedo Hernández, Antonio. <u>Teatro</u>. Santiago : Editorial Nascimento, 1927-1934)

0/14   Acevedo Hernández, Antonio. <u>Comedias</u>. (Santiago : Editorial Nascimento, 1932-33)

0/15   Aguilera Malta, Demetrio. <u>No bastan los átomos</u>.... (Quito : Editorial Casa de la Cultura Ecuadoriana, 1955)

0/16   Alvarez Lleras, Antonio. <u>Obras dramáticas de Antonio Alvarez Lleras</u>. (Bogotá : Imp. J. Casis, 192?)

0/17   Alvarez Lleras, Antonio. Víboras sociales....
        (Bogotá : Editorial Minerva, 1936)
0/18   Ayala Michelena, Leopoldo. Dánosle hoy....
        (Caracas : Editorial Tamanaco, 1941)
0/19   Ayala Michelena, Leopoldo. Al dejar las mu-
        ñecas.... (Caracas : Tip. La Nación, 1934)
0/20   Bengoa, Juan León. Tres dramas. (Montevideo :
        Editorial Letras, 1952)
0/21   Bloch, Pedro. Teatro. (Rio : Irmãos Pongetti,
        1961)
0/22   Díez Barroso, Victor Manuel. Siete obras en un
        acto. (México : Imprenta Mundial, 1935)
0/23   Camargo, Joracy. Teatro. (São Paulo : Martins,
        1961)
0/24   Capdevila, Arturo. Amor de Schahrazada....
        (3rd ed. , Buenos Aires : Cabaut & Cia. ,
        1928)
0/25   Camargo, Joracy. Deus lhe pague. (Rio : Liv-
        raria Educadora, 193?)
0/26   Bustillo Oro, Juan. Tres dramas mexicanas.
        (Madrid : Editôra Cenit, 1933)
0/27   Fabregat Cúneo, Roberto. Teatro. (Montevideo :
        Ediciones Universo, 1952)
0/29   Elorduy, Aquiles. `Comedias mexicanas. (Méx-
        ico, 1953)
0/30   Los tres: Pedro E. Pico, R. González Pacheco,
        Samuel Eichelbaum.... (Buenos Aires :
        M. Gleizer, 1928)
0/31   Eichelbaum, Samuel. Un tal Servando Gómez....
        (Buenos Aires : Ediciones Conducta, 1942)
0/32   Eichelbaum, Samuel. Soledad es tu nombre....
        (Buenos Aires : M. Gleizer, 1932)
0/33   3 comedias para el teatro infantil. (México :
        Secretaría de Educación Pública, 1935)
0/34   Eichelbaum, Samuel. Un monstruo en libertad.
        (Buenos Aires : M. Gleizer, 1925)
0/35   Galigh, Manuel. Obras de teatro. (Guatemala :
        Ministerio de Educación Pública, 1953)
0/36   Gamboa, José Joaquín. Teatro. (México : Botas,
        1938)
0/37   González Pacheco, Rodolfo. Teatro completo.
        (Buenos Aires : Editorial Americalee, 1953)
0/38   González Paredes, Ramón. Samuel y Ellos.
        (Caracas : Tip. Garrido, 1947)
0/41   Guizado, Rafael. Cinco veces amor. (Bogotá :
        Libreria Suramerica, 1948)
0/42   Ibarbourou, Juana de. Obras completas. (Mad-
        rid : Aguilar, 1953)

0/43   Innes-González, Eduardo. Teatro. (Caracas :
        Tip. Americana, 1935)
0/44   Larreta, Enrique Rodríguez. Obras completas.
        (Madrid : Plenitud, 1958)
0/45   Larreta, Enrique Rodríguez. Jerónimo y su
        almohada, y Notas.... (2nd ed. , Buenos
        Aires : Espasa-Calpe Argentina, 1946)
0/46   Larreta, Enrique Rodríguez. La que buscaba
        Don Juan.... (Buenos Aires : L. J. Rosso,
        1938)
0/47   Larreta, Enrique Rodríguez. La que buscaba Don
        Juan, Artemis.... (Buenos Aires : Espasa-
        Calpe Argentina, 1945)
0/49   Larreta, Enrique Rodríguez. Santa María del
        Buen Aire. Tiempos iluminados. (Buenos
        Aires : Espasa-Calpe Argentina, 1941)
0/50   List Arzubide, Germán. Tres obras del teatro
        revolucionario de Germán List Arzubide.
        (México : Ediciones Integrales, 1933)
0/51   Macau, Miguel A. Soledad.... (La Habana :
        Cultural, 1933)
0/52   Macau, Miguel A. Teatro. (La Habana : Com-
        pañía Impresora Industrial, 1924)
0/53   Macau, Miguel A. Teatro. (La Habana : Albino
        Rodríguez, 1937)
0/54   Magalhães, Paulo de. Comedias de Paulo de Mag-
        alhães. (São Paulo : V. Pontes, 1952)
0/56   Martí, José. Teatro. (La Habana : Trópico,
        1940)
0/57   Martínez Cuitiño, Vicente. La Fuerza ciega.
        La humilde quimera. (Buenos Aires : M.
        Gleizer, 1923)
0/58   Martínez Cuitiño, Vicente. La Mala siempre....
        (Buenos Aires : M. Gleizer, 1924)
0/59   Martínez Cuitiño, Vicente. Teatro. (2 vols. ,
        Buenos Aires : M. Gleizer, 1923-24)
0/60   Martínez, José de Jesús. La Mentira, drama.
        (Madrid : Murillo, 1954)
0/61   Méndez Ballester, Manuel. El Clamor de los
        surcos y Tiempo muerte. (México : Orión,
        1955)
0/62   Mesquita, Alfredo. 3 peças. (São Paulo : Edi-
        tôra Spes, 1937)
0/63   Mondragón Aguirre, Magdalena. 2 obras de te-
        atro. (México : Grupo América, 1951)
0/64   Moock Bousquet, Armando. Teatro seleccionado,
        vol. 2. (Santiago : Editorial Cultura, 1937)

0/65   Ortiz Guerrero, Manuel. Obras completas. (Asunción : Editorial Indoamericana, 1952)

0/66   Othón, Manuel José. Obras completas. (México : Nueva España, 1945)

0/67   Ozores, Renato. Teatro. (Panamá : Editora Panamá América, 1954)

0/68   Pacheco, Carlos Mauricio. Don Quijano de la pampa.... (Buenos Aires : Bambalinas, 1922)

0/69   Pagano, José León. El Hombre que volvió a la vida. (Buenos Aires : M. Gleizer, 1922)

0/70   Payró, Roberto J. Teatro. (Buenos Aires : J. Menéndez, 1925)

0/71   Penna, Luiz Carlos Martins. Teatro comico. (São Paulo : Cultura, 1943)

0/72   Pico, Pedro E. La Novia de los forasteros.... (Buenos Aires : M. Gleizer, 1928)

0/73   Princivalle, Carlos Maria. Teatro de Princivalle. (Montevideo : Editorial "La Facultad," M. García, 1929)

0/74   Rendón, Victor Manuel. Obras dramáticas de Victor Manuel Rendón. (Paris : Livre Libre, 1927)

0/75   Rodríguez, Yamandú. Fraile Aldao. (Montevideo : García, 1935)

0/76   Sánchez, Florencio. Barranca abajo. (Barcelona : Cervantes, 1926)

0/77   Sánchez, Florencio. Barranca abajo, Los muertos. (Buenos Aires : L. J. Rosso, 1939)

0/78   Sánchez, Florencio. Canillita y Cedulas. (Buenos Aires : L. Bernard, 1921)

0/79   Sánchez, Florencio. Los derechos de la salud.... (Valencia : Editorial Cervantes, 1920)

0/80   Plays of the Southern Americas. (Stanford University, 1942)

0/81   Sánchez, Florencio. M'hijo el dotor.... (Buenos Aires : Cóndor, 1939)

0/82   Sánchez, Florencio. Los muertos.... (Buenos Aires : Cóndor, 1939)

0/83   Sánchez, Florencio. El Teatro del uruguayo Florencio Sánchez.... (Barcelona : Cervantes, 1926; 3 vols.)

0/84   Sánchez, Florencio. Teatro. (Montevideo : C. García, 1936)

0/85   Sánchez, Florencio. Teatro. (Buenos Aires : Sopena, 1944)

0/86   Sánchez, Florencio. Théatre choisi. (Paris, 1939)

0/87   Sánchez, Florencio. Teatro completo. (Buenos
         Aires : Claridad, 1941)
0/88   Sánchez Galarraga, Gustavo. Teatro. (La Ha-
         bana, 1920; 5 vols.)
0/89   Three plays of the Argentine. Ed. by Edward
         Hale Bierstadt. (New York : Duffield, 1920)
0/90   Segura, Manuel Ascension. Comedias. (Lima :
         Garcilaso, 1924)
0/91   Spota, Luis. Dos obras de teatro. (México :
         Secretaría de Educación Pública, 1949)
0/92   Urueta, Margarita. San Lunes, Una hora de
         vida.... (México : Quetzal, 1943)
0/93   Vacarezza, Alberto. Cuentos cortos, colección
         en un acto. (Buenos Aires : La Escena,
         1920)
0/94   Vargas Tejada, Luis. Las Convulsiones y Dora-
         minta. (Bogotá : Minerva, 1935)
0/96   Yunque, Alvaro. Miguel cantó. Somos hermanos.
         (Buenos Aires : Teatro del Pueblo, 1936)
0/97   Yunque, Alvaro. 7 obras de teatro para niños.
         (Buenos Aires : Occidente, 1941)
0/98   Penna, Luiz Carlos Martins. Comedias. (Rio :
         H. Garnier, 1929)
0/99   Magdaleno, Mauricio Teatro revolucionario mex-
         icano. (Madrid : Cenit, 1933)
0/101   Best short plays, 1959/60. Ed. by Margaret
         Gardner Mayarga (Boston : Beacon, 1959)
0/102   Teatro cubano contemporáneo. Ed. by Luis A.
         Baralt. (Madrid : Aguilar, 1959)
0/103   Belaval, Emilio S. Areyto. (San Juan : Biblio-
         teca de Autores Puertorriqueños, 1948)
1/2116   Montalvo, Juan. El Libro de las pasiones (La
         Habana : Ed. cultural, 1935)
1/2117   Pérez Taylor, Rafael. Del Hampa. Teatro
         sintético. (México, 1935)
3/3328   Macau, Miguel A. Obras dramaticas. (La Ha-
         bana : Hermes, 193?)
3/3329   Moock, Armando. Teatro seleccionado, vol. 1.
         (Santiago : Cultura, 1937)
3/3330   Rendón, Victor Manuel. Teatro. Obras repre-
         sentadas en el Ecuador, 1920-1936. (Guaya-
         quil : Reed & Reed, 1937)
4/3980   Azuela, Mariano. Teatro. (México : Botas, 1938)
5/3970   Faia, Octávio de. Três tragédias à sombra da
         cruz. (Rio : José Olympio, 1938)
5/3974   Magalhães Júnior, Raymundo. O Homen que fica
         e A mulher que todos querem. (Rio : A
         Noite, 1939)

6/4410	Silva, Antonio José da. <u>Amphytrião; ou, Jupiter e Alcmena, e Guerras do alecrim e mangerona.</u> (Rio : A Noite, 1939)
7/4708	Cortinas, Ismael. <u>Teatro.</u> (Montevideo : C. García, 1941)
7/4709	Innes-González, Eduardo. <u>La Virgen del carmen y Vivir para los demás.</u> (Caracas : Ed. Elite, 1941)
7/4990	Caraco, Alberto. <u>Inès de Castro, Les martyrs de Cordoue</u> (Rio : Livr. General Franco-brasileira, 1941)
9/3950	Villaurrutia, Xavier. <u>Autos profanos.</u> (México : Ed. Letras de México, 1943)
9/4298	Pena, Martins. <u>Teatro cômico.</u> (São Paulo : Ed. Cultura, 1943)
10/3679	Larreta, Enrique Rodríguez. <u>El "Linyera"; Pasión de Roma.</u> (Buenos Aires : Espasa-Calpe Argentina, 1944)
11/3331	Gutiérrez Hermosillo, Alfonso. <u>Teatro.</u> (México : Ed. de la Universidad Nacional Autónoma, 1945)
11/3332	Ibarbourou, Juana de. <u>Los Sueños de Natacha. Cinco obras de teatro para niños.</u> (Montevideo : Ed. Liceo, 1945)
11/3338	Nalé Roxlo, Conrado. <u>El Pacto de Cristina....</u> (Buenos Aires : Losada, 1945)
12/2750	Galich, Manuel. <u>Obras de teatro.</u> (Guatemala : Tip. Nacional, 1946)
12/2752	Genta, Walter Homero. <u>Humanidad.</u> (Montevideo : Ed. Florensa & Lafon, 1946)
12/2753	Ghiraldo, Alberto. <u>Teatro Argentino.</u> (Buenos Aires : Americalee, 1946)
12/2765	<u>Teatro folklore nicaragüense.</u> Ed. by Francisco Pérez Estrada. (Managua : Nuevos Horizontes, 1946)
12/2766	<u>Teatro escolar.</u> (Lima : Ministerio de Educación Pública, 1946)
12/2768	<u>Teatro mexicano. Dos obras de un acto.</u> Ed. by Fernando Wagner. (México : Secretaría de Educación Pública, 1946)
12/2938	Bofanini, Darcília Azarany. <u>Almas e destinos. Pecas radio-teatrais.</u> (Rio : Zélio Valverde, 194?)
13/2227	Correa, Pancho. <u>Teatro.</u> (Montevideo : Florensa & Lafón, 1947)
13/2231	García Velloso, Enrique. <u>Mamá Culepina; La Cadena....</u> (Buenos Aires : A. Estrada, 1947)

13/2234   López Crespo, Iris de. Teatro. (Montevideo :
          Editorial Prisma, 1947)
13/2235   Mondragón Aguirre, Magdalena. Cuando Eva se
          vuelve Adán y Torbellino. (México : Secre-
          taría de Educación Pública, 1947)
14/2960   Orrego Vicuña, Eugenio. Ensayos dramáticos.
          (Santiago : Universidad de Chile, 1948)
14/2966   Teatro Peruano contemporáneo. Ed. by Aurelio
          Miro Quesada Sosa. (Lima : Huascarán,
          1948)
14/3076   Rodrigues, Nelson. Anjo negro. Vestido de
          noiva. A mulher sem pecado. (Rio : Cruz-
          eiro, 1948)
15/2434   Acuña, Manuel. Obras. (México : Porrua, 194?)
15/2438   Galich, Manuel. Historia a escena, La. (Guate-
          mala : Ministerio de Educación Pública,
          1949)
15/2441   Manet, Eduardo. Scherzo. (La Habana : Ed-
          iciones Prometeo, 194?)
15/2444   Sierra, Justo. Obras completas, vol. 2. (Méx-
          ico : UNAM, 1948)
16/2781   Amorim, Enrique. La Segunda sangre....
          (Buenos Aires : Conducta, 1950)
16/2782   Ayala Michelena, Leopoldo. Teatro seleccionado.
          (Caracas : El Creyón, 1950)
16/2789   Macau, Miguel. Obras dramaticas. (México,
          1950)
16/2790   México en escena. Ed. by Tomas Perrin. (Méx-
          ico : Excélsior, 1950)
16/2916   Anchieta, José de. Na vila de Vitória.... (São
          Paulo : Museu Paulista, 1950)
17/2554   Certad, Aquiles. Tres obras de teatro. (Buenos
          Aires : Editorial Interamericana, 1951)
17/2557   Dow, Alberto. La Sangre petrificada.... (Bo-
          gotá : Spiral, 1951)
17/2562   Sánchez, Florencio. Teatro completo. (Buenos
          Aires : El Ateneo, 1951)
17/2649   Pena, Martins. O Juiz de paz na roca....
          (Rio : Simões, 1951)
18/2683   Eichelbaum, Samuel. El gato y su selva....
          (Buenos Aires : Editorial Sudamericana,
          1952)
18/2684   Feder, Carlos Eduardo. Teatro para leer.
          (Buenos Aires : Imprenta López, 1952)
18/2685   Fein, María Teresa. Teatro. (Montevideo :
          Imprenta Letras, 1952)
18/2686   Ferreti, Aurelio. Farsas. (Buenos Aires : Ting-
          lado, 1952)

18/2690   Laferrère, Gregorio de. Teatro completo. (San-
            ta Fe, Argentina : Castellví, 1952)
18/2693   Matorras Cornejo, Carlos. Cuando Zeus está
            ausente. (Buenos Aires : Ediciones de La
            Carpa, 1952)
18/2695   Sánchez, Florencio. Teatro completo. (Buenos
            Aires : Claridad, 1952)
18/2698   Teatro para escolares y aficionados. Ed. by
            Ruben Sotoconil. (Santiago : Ernesto Toro,
            1952)
18/2701   Yunque, Alvaro. Un diamante en el apéndice....
            (Buenos Aires : Quetzal, 1952)
18/2815   Benedetti, Luica. O Banquete. (Rio : Sociedade
            Brasileira de Autores Teatrais, 1952)
19/5151   Arriví, Francisco. Una Sombra menos.... (Mad-
            rid : Talleres gráficos Méndez, 1953)
19/5152   Blanco-Amor, Eduardo. Farsas. (Buenos Aires :
            López Negri, 1953)
19/5171   Plaza Noblia, Héctor. Teatro de cámara....
            (Montevideo : Gaceta Comercial, 1954)
19/5177   Villaurrutia, Xavier. Poesía y teatro completos.
            (México : Fondo de Cultura Económica, 1953)
19/5380   Brierre, Jean F. Pétion y Bolívar.... (Buenos
            Aires : Ediciones Troquel, 1955)
20/4200   Alfonso, Paco. Yari-yari; teatro. (La Habana :
            La Milagrosa, 1956)
20/4201   Teatro hispanoamericano. Ed. by Hymen Alpern
            and José Martel. (New York : Odyssey
            Press, 1956)
20/4212   Carlino, Carlos. La Biunda.... (Buenos Aires :
            Ediciones del Instituto Amigos del Libro
            Argentino, 1955)
20/4217   García, Juan Agustín. Obras completas. (Buenos
            Aires : Zamora, 1955)
20/4224   Payró, Roberto J. Teatro completo. (Buenos
            Aires : Librería Hachette, 1956)
20/4227   Plaza, Angélica. La Tierra ilimitada. (Monte-
            video : Letras, 1954)
20/4228   Rapoport, Nicolás. Teatro. (Buenos Aires :
            Losange, 1955)
20/4231   Sánchez Gardel, Julio. Teatro. (Buenos Aires :
            Hachette, 1955)
20/4234   Teatro mexicano del siglo XX. (México : Fondo
            de Cultura Económica, 1956)
20/4418   Accioly Netto, A. Três máscaras. (Rio : O
            Cruzeiro, 1956)
20/4423   Vianna, Renato. Obras completas, vol. 1.
            (Rio : A Noite, 1954)

21/4206   Borges, Jorge Luis and Bioy Casares, Adolfo.
           Los Orilleros.... (Buenos Aires : Losada,
           1955)
21/4208   Carballido, Emilio. La Hebra de oro.... (Méx-
           ico : Imp. Universitaria, 1957)
21/4209   El Sainete criollo. Ed. by Tullio Carella.
           (Buenos Aires : Hachette, 1957)
21/4210   Concurso Nacional de Teatro : Obras Premiadas,
           1954-1955. (México : Instituto Nacional de
           Bellas Artes, 1956)
21/4216   Gallegos, Rómulo. La Doncella.... (México :
           Ediciones Montobar, 1957)
21/4218   Gorostiza, Manuel Eduardo de. Teatro selecto.
           (México : Porrua, 1957)
21/4223   Nalé Roxlo, Conrado La Cola de la sirena....
           (Buenos Aires : Editorial Sudamericana,
           1957)
21/4227   Dos obras. Carlos Prieto and Carlos Solórzano.
           (México : Col. Teatro Mexicano, 1957)
21/4228   Romero de Terreros, Manuel. Teatro breve.
           (México : Los Presentes, 1956)
21/4229   Rosenrauch, E. 3 dramas. (Santiago : Universo,
           1956)
21/4234   Vera, Pedro Jorge. Teatro. (Quito : Casa de la
           Cultura Ecuatoriana, 1956)
21/4326   Borba Filho, Hermilo. Teatro. (Recife : Ed-
           ições TEP, 1952)
21/4327   Fernades, Millôr. Teatro de Millôr Fernandes.
           (Rio : Civilização Brasileira, 1957)
21/4328   Kelly, Celso. Encruzilhadas. (Rio : Edições
           G. T. L., 195?)
21/4329   Machado, Maria Clara. Teatro infantil. (Rio :
           AGIR, 1957)
22/5310   Garro, Elena. Un Hogar sólido y otras piezas
           en un acto. (Xalapa : Universidad Veracruz-
           ana, 1958)
22/5312   Teatro gauchesco primitivo. Ed. by Juan Carlos
           Ghiano. (Buenos Aires : Losange, 1957)
22/5315   Antología del teatro hispanoamericano. Ed. by
           Willis K. Jones. (México : Andrea, 1959)
22/5318   Martínez Estrada, Ezequiel. Tres dramas.
           (Buenos Aires : Losange, 1957)
22/5319   Mediz Bolio, Antonio. Teatro social. (México :
           Universidad Nacional del Sureste, 1956)
22/5322   Páez, Leonardo. La Bruma frente al espejo....
           (Quito : Casa de la Cultura Ecuatoriana,
           1957)

22/5327   Silva Valdés, Fernán. Santos Vega.... (Buenos
           Aires : Losada, 1957)
22/5329   Teatro en un acto. Ed. by Rubén Sotoconil.
           (Santiago : Nascimento, 1957)
22/5334   Uslar Pietri, Arturo. Teatro. (Caracas : Ed-
           iciones EDIME, 1958)
22/5525   Bloch, Pedro. As Mãos de Eurídice.... (Rio :
           Civilização Brasileira, 1957)
22/5527   Penna, Luíz Carlos Martins. Teatro. (Rio :
           Ministério da Educação e Cultura, Instituto
           Nacional do Livro, 1956; 2 vols.)
22/5528   Seljan, Zora. 3 Mulheres de Xangô. (Rio :
           Edições GRD, 1958)
22/5529   Silva, Antônio José da. A Vida de Esopo....
           (Rio : Civilização Brasileira, 1957)
23/5300   Aguilera Malta, Demetrio. Trilogía ecuatoriana.
           (México : Ediciones De Andrea, 1959)
23/5307   Barros Grez, Daniel. El Casi casamiento....
           (Santiago : Editorial del Nuevo Extremo,
           1959)
23/5309   Teatro argentino contemporáneo. Ed. by Arturo
           Berenguer Carisomo. (Madrid : Aguilar,
           1959)
23/5311   Calderón, Fernando. Dramas y poesías. (Méx-
           ico : Porrua, 1959)
23/5313   Carballido, Emilio. Teatro. (México : Fondo de
           Cultura Económica, 1960)
23/5315   Crimi, Humberto. El Actor.... (Mendoza, Ar-
           gentina : Ediciones Biblioteca San Martín, 1959)
23/5317   Domínguez, Franklin. El Ultimo instante....
           (Ciudad Trujillo, 1958)
23/5318   Marionetas. Ed. by Franklin Domínguez, a. o.
           (Ciudad Trujillo : Editora Librería Domin-
           icana, 1958)
23/5331   Marqués, René. Los Soles truncos.... (Méx-
           ico : Ediciones Arrecife, 1959)
23/5336   Palino, Piquio. Tres farsas de actualidad para
           teatro, cine o radio. (Buenos Aires, 1956)
23/5342   Solórzano, Cárlos. Tres actos. (México : El
           Unicornio, 1959)
23/5343   Teatro mexicano, 1958. (México : Aguilar, 1959)
23/5344   Teatro puertorriqueño. (San Juan : Instituto de
           Cultura Puertorriqueña, 1959)
23/5346   Tres obras de teatro. (Managua : Academia Nic-
           caragüense de la Lengua, 1957)
23/5348   Primera antología de obras en un acto. Ed. by
           Maruxa Vilalta. (México : Colección Teatro
           Mexicano, 1959)

24/5600   Araujo, Gonzalo. Nada bajo el ciel-raso....
           (Medellín, 1960)
24/5601   Arriví, Francisco. Bolero y plena. (San Juan :
           Tinglado Puertorriqueño, 1960)
24/5607   Carlino, Carlos. Un Cabello sobre la almo-
           hada.... (Buenos Aires : Ediciones Cátedra
           Lisandro de la Torre, 1958)
24/5608   Cuzzani, Agustín. Teatro. (Buenos Aires :
           Quetzal, 1960)
24/5609   Discépolo, Armando. Tres grotescos. (Buenos
           Aires : Ediciones Losange, 1958)
24/5612   Tres piezas breves. Ed. by Víctor Fabiani a. o.
           (Buenos Aires, 1960)
24/5618   Larreta, Enrique. Dramáticas personas. (Buen-
           os Aires : Kraft, 1959)
24/5621   Mendoza Gutiérrez, Alfredo. Nuestro teatro
           campesino. (México : Centro Regional de
           Educación Fundamental para la América
           Latina, 1960)
24/5623   Molleto Labarca, Enrique. Un Cambio importante.
           (Santiago : Editorial del Pacífico, 1960)
24/5624   Mota, Fernando. La Llave y otras obras. (Méx-
           ico : Editorial Estaciones, 1960)
24/5626   El Drama rural. Ed. by Luis Ordaz. (Buenos
           Aires : Librería Hachette, 1959)
24/5627   Siete sainetes porteños. Ed. by Luis Ordaz.
           (Buenos Aires : Losange, 1958)
24/5632   Salinas Pérez, Pablo. Los Hombrecillos de
           gris.... (México, 1959)
24/5633   Segura, Manuel Ascensio. El Sargento Canuto....
           (Lima : Editorial Nuevos Rumbos, 1958)
24/5635   Solana, Rafael. Espada en mano. (México, 1960)
24/5638   Teatro mexicano contemporáneo. (Madrid : Aguil-
           ar, 1959)
24/5639   Teatro puertorriqueño : segundo festival. (San
           Juan : Instituto de Cultura Puertorriqueña,
           1960)
24/5640   Teatro uruguayo contemporáneo. (Madrid :
           Aguilar, 1960)
24/5643   Segunda antología de obras en un acto. (México,
           1960)
24/5644   Tercera antología de obras en un acto. (México,
           1960)
24/5796   Andrade, Jorge. Pedreira das Almas.... (Rio :
           AGIR, 1960)
25/4557   Bernal, Rafael. Antonia.... (México : Jus, 1960)

25/4561   Cogolani, Roberto Dante. Perfiles para la
           muerte. (Buenos Aires : Ediciones del
           Carro de Tespis, 1960)
25/4566   Larreta, Enrique. Obras completas. (Buenos
           Aires : Ediciones Antonio Zamora, 1959; 2
           vols.)
25/4568   Los Linares. . . . Ed. by Andrés Lizárraga.
           (Buenos Aires : Talía, 1960)
25/4570   Mombrú, María. El Andén y dos monólogos.
           (La Plata, Argentina : Ediciones del Min-
           isterio de Educación, 1957)
25/4571   3 Obras dramáticas de Cuba revolucionaria. Ed.
           by Matias de Montes Huidobro. (La Ha-
           bana : Instituto de Cultura de Marianao,
           1961)
25/4574   Piñera, Virgilio. Teatro completo. (La Ha-
           bana : Ediciones Revolución, 1960)
25/4576   Sánchez, Luis Rafael. Los Angeles se han
           fatigado. . . . (Barcelona : Ediciones Lugar,
           1960)
25/4582   Teatro puertorriqueño. Tercer festival. (San
           Juan : Instituto de Cultura Puertorriqueña,
           1961)
25/4584   Wainer, Alberto. Teatro. (Buenos Aires : M.
           Gleizer, 1959)
25/4727   Peixoto, Maria Luiza Amaral. Velório amigo.
           Teatro. (Rio : Edições GRD, 1961)
25/4728   Pena, Luis Carlos Martins. Comédias. (Rio :
           Jornal do Brasil, 1927)
25/4729   Rodrigues, Nelson. Teatro. (Rio : Serviço
           Nacional de Teatro, 1959-60; 2 vols.)
26/1830   Argüelles, Hugo. Teatro. (México : Ediciones
           Oasis, 1961)
26/1833   Arrufat, Antón. Teatro. (La Habana : Ediciones
           Unión-Teatro, 1963)
26/1839   Buenaventura, Enrique. Teatro. (Bogotá : Ed-
           iciones Tercer Mundo, 1963)
26/1840   Canal Feijóo, Bernardo. Los Casos de Juan.
           (Buenos Aires : Talía, 1961)
26/1842   Carballido, Emilio. D. F. , 14 obras en un acto.
           (Mexico : Univ. Veracruzana, 1962)
26/1849   Deugenio, Rubén. Quiniela. . . . (Montevideo :
           Editorial El Siglo Ilustrado, 1962)
26/1851   Felipe, Carlos. Teatro. (Santa Clara : Uni-
           versidad de Las Villas, 1959)
26/1852   Teatro cubano. Ed. by Carlos Felipe a. o.
           (Santa Clara : Universidad de Las Villas, 1960)

26/1854   Ferrer, Rolando. Teatro. (La Habana : Ed-
          iciones Unión-Teatro, 1963)
26/1857   Gamarra, Abelardo M. Teatro. (Huamachuco,
          Peru : Centro Cultural Sánchez Carrión,
          1961)
26/1858   Gramcko, Ida. Teatro. (Caracas : Ministerio de
          Educación, 1961)
26/1860   Heiremans, Luis Alberto. Versos de ciego.
          (Santiago, 1962)
26/1863   Junio 16 .... Ed. by Néstor Kraly. (Buenos
          Aires : Ediciones Nueva Visión, 1961)
26/1864   Leguizamón, Martiniano. Calandria.... (Buenos
          Aires : Ediciones Solar-Hachette, 1961)
26/1866   Lizárraga, Andrés. Teatro. (Buenos Aires :
          Editôra Quetzal, 1962)
26/1871   Ríos, Juan. Teatro, vol. 1. (Lima : Libreria
          Editorial J. Mejía Baca, 1961)
26/1876   Salazar Bondy, Sebastián. Teatro. (Buenos
          Aires : Losada, 1961)
26/1880   Teatro bufo. (La Habana : Universidad Central
          de Las Villas, 1961)
26/1881   Teatro cubano. (La Habana : Casa de las Amér-
          icas, 1961)
26/1882   Teatro mexicano, 1959. (México : Aguilar Editor,
          1962)
26/1883   Teatro puertorriqueño, cuarto festival. (San
          Juan : Instituto de Cultura Puertorriqueña,
          1962)
26/1885   Triana, José. El Parque de la fraternidad. (La
          Habana : Ediciones Unión-Teatro, 1962)
26/2076   Gomes, Alfredo Dias. A Invasão.... (Rio : Ed-
          itôra Civilização Brasileira, 1962)
28/2265   Buitrago, Fanny. Hombre de paja.... (Bogota :
          Espiral, 1964)
28/2277   Costantini, Humberto. 3 Monólogos. (Buenos
          Aires : Falbo, 1964)
28/2280   Díaz Díaz, Oswaldo. Teatro, vol. 1. (Bogotá :
          Publicaciones Editoriales, 1963)
28/2284   Dragún, Osvaldo. Teatro. (Buenos Aires : G.
          Dávalos, 1965)
28/2285   Milagro en el mercado viejo.... Ed. by Osvaldo
          Dragún a. o. (La Habana : Casa de las
          Américas, 1963)
28/2287   Fernández de Lizardi, José. Obras de Fernández
          de Lizardi. (México : Centro de Estudios
          Literarios, 1965)
28/2288   Ferrari Amores, Alfonso. A la sombra del alto
          manzano.... (Buenos Aires : Tespis, 1965)

28/2289   Ferreti, Aurelio.   Teatro.   (Buenos Aires : Quet-
          zal, 1963)
28/2290   Teatro Puertorriqueño: quinto festival.   (San Juan :
          Instituto de Cultura Puertorriqueña, 1963)
28/2291   Festival de Teatro Puertorriqueño, VI.   (San
          Juan : Instituto de Cultura Puertorriqueña,
          1964)
28/2292   Festival de Teatro Puertorriqueño, VII.   (San
          Juan : Instituto de Cultura Puertorriqueña,
          1965)
28/2293   García de Paredes, Carlos M.   El Minotauro....
          (Panamá : Imprenta Nacional, 1963)
28/2301   Cuarta antología de obras de un acto.   Ed. by
          Luisa Josefina Hernández a. o.   (México :
          Peregrina, 1965)
28/2301   Ibargüengoitia, Jorge.   Clotilde....   (Xalapa :
          Universidad Veracruzana, 1964)
28/2304   Laferrère, Gregorio de.   Jettatore....   (Buenos
          Aires : Editorial Universitaria de Buenos
          Aires, 1964)
28/2312   Milanés, José Jacinto.   Obras completas, vol. 1.
          (La Habana : Editora del Consejo Nacional
          de Cultura, 1963)
28/2315   Nalé Roxlo, Conrado.   Teatro breve.   (Buenos
          Aires : Editorial Huemul, 1964)
28/2323   Osorio, Luis Enrique.   Teatro, vols. 3 and 4.
          (Bogotá : Ediciones de la Idea, 1963-64)
28/2325   Pellegrini, Aldo.   Teatro de la inestable realidad.
          (Buenos Aires : Tespis, 1964)
28/2332   Silvain, Julio César.   3 Días con gerente.
          (Buenos Aires : Sirocco, 1965)
28/2339   Usigli, Rodolfo.   Teatro completo, vol. 1.   (Méx-
          ico : Fondo de Cultura Económica, 1963)
28/2388a Teatro guatemalteco.   (Madrid : Aguilar, 1964)
28/2388b El Teatro hispanoamericano contemporáneo.   (Méx-
          ico : Fondo de Cultura Económica, 1964; 2
          vols.)
28/2654   Teatro brasileiro contemporâneo.   Ed. by Wilson
          Martins a. o.   (New York : Appleton-
          Century-Crofts, 1966)
28/2656   Teatro costumbrista brasileño.   Ed. by Martins
          Pena a. o.   (Rio : Ministério da Educação
          e Cultura, Instituto Nacional do Livro, 1961)

List of Periodicals Indexed

[Whenever possible, the alphabetic codes correspond to those in the Handbook of Latin American Studies.]

AM/R	Revista do Arquivo Municipal. São Paulo, Brazil.
AMERICA	América. México.
ANHEMBI	Anhembi. São Paulo, Brazil.
AVANT	Avant-Scène Théatre. Paris, France.
B INST RIVA AGUERO	Boletín del Instituto Reva-Agüero. Lima, Peru. Pontifica Universidad Católica del Perú.
BAMBAL	Bambalinas. Buenos Aires, Argentina.
BOL ESTUD TEATRO	Boletin de Estudios de Teatro. Buenos Aires, Argentina.
CAM	Cuadernos Americanos. México.
CCE/R	Revista. Quito, Ecuador. Casa de la Cultura Ecuatoriana.
CDLA	Casa de las Américas. La Habana, Cuba.
CDLA/CO	Conjunto. Revista de teatro latino-americano. La Habana, Cuba. Casa de las Américas.
CLA	Clã. Revista de cultura. Fortaleza, Brazil.
COLEGIO	Colégio. São Paulo, Brazil.
CUBN/R	Revista de la Biblioteca Nacional. La Habana, Cuba
CULT U	Cultura Universitaria. Caracas, Venezuela.
ENTREACTO	El Entreacto. Buenos Aires, Argentina.
ES	Estaciones. Revista literaria de México. México.

ESCENA	La Escena. Revista teatral. Buenos Aires, Argentina.
EXCELSIOR	Excelsior. Revista semanal de literatura. Santiago, Chile.
F	Ficción. Revista-Libro Bimestral. Buenos Aires, Argentina. Editorial Goyanarte.
FRANCE ILLUSTRATION	France Illustration. Paris, France.
HIJO PRODIGO	Hijo Pródigo. México.
HORA	Hora del Hombre. Lima, Peru.
IJACI/C	Comentario. Buenos Aires, Argentina. Instituto Judío Argentino de Cultura e Información.
INBA/CBA	Cuadernos de Bellas Artes. México. Instituto Nacional de Bellas Artes.
INBA/R	Revista de la Escuela de Arte Teatral. México. Instituto Nacional de Bellas Artes
LET MEX	Letras de México. México.
MAGN/B	Boletín del Archivo General de la Nación. México.
MAR DEL SUR	Mar del Sur. Revista peruana de cultura. Lima, Peru.
MER PER	Mercurio Peruano. Lima, Peru.
MEX ARTE	México en el Arte. México.
MORADAS	Moradas. Revista de las artes y de las letras. Lima, Peru.
N	Número. Montevideo, Uruguay.
NOSOTROS	Nosotros. Buenos Aires, Argentina.
NUEVA GEN	Nueva Generación. La Habana, Cuba.
PAN	Panoramas. México.
PANOR TEAT MEX	Panorama del Teatro de México. México.
PAU/AM	Americas. Washington, DC, USA. Pan American Union. (English edition)
PEGASO	Pegaso. Montevideo, Uruguay.
POET LORE	Poet Lore. Boston, MA, USA.
PRIA	Primer Acto. Revista de Teatro. Madrid, Spain.
PROMETEO	Prometeo. Revista de divulgación teatral. La Habana, Cuba.
PROV SAO PEDRO	Provincia de São Pedro. Pôrto Alegre, Brazil.

R LYCEUM	Revista Lyceum. La Habana, Cuba.
REG CULT YUC	Regístro de Cultura Yucateca. México
REV ACAD BRAS LET	Revista da Academia Brasileira de Letras. Rio de Janeiro, Brazil.
REV AMERICA	Revista de América. Bogotá, Columbia.
REV GUAT	Revista de Guatemala. Guatemala.
REV INDIAS	Revista de las Indias. Bogotá, Columbia.
REV MIN CULT	Revista del Ministerio de Cultura. San Salvador, El Salvador.
RML	Revista Mexicana de Literatura. México. Libros de México.
RTB	Revista de Teatro. Rio de Janeiro, Brazil. Sociedade Brasileira de Autores (SBAT). Formerly known as SBAT Boletim.
RUECA	Rueca. México.
TALIA	Talía. Revista de teatro y artes. Buenos Aires, Argentina.
TEAT ARG	El Teatro Argentino. Buenos Aires, Argentina.
TEAT BR	Teatro Brazileiro. São Paulo, Brazil.
TEAT NAC	El Teatro Nacional. Buenos Aires, Argentina.
TEAT POP	Teatro Popular. Buenos Aires, Argentina.
TEAT UN CHILE	Teatro. Teatro experimental. Santiago, Chile. Universidad de Chile.
TEATRO	Teatro. Madrid, Spain.
TIERRA NUEVA	Tierra Nueva. Revista de Letras Universitarias.
UCC/FT	Finis Terrae. Revista Trimestral. Santiago, Chile. Universidad Católica de Chile. Dep. de Extension Cultural.
UCCH/A	Apuntes. Revista de teatro de la Universidad Católica de Chile. Santiago, Chile.
UCH/A	Anales de la Universidad de Chile. Santiago, Chile.
UMIP/RN	Revista Nacional. Montevideo, Uruguay. Ministerio de Instrucción Pública.

UNAM/UM	Universidad de México. Revista de la Universidad de México. México. Universidad Nacional Autómona de México.
UNIV HABANA	Universidad de la Habana. La Habana, Cuba.
UNIV NAC COL	Universidad Nacional de Colombia. Revista trimestral de cultura moderna. Bogotá, Columbia.
UNIV PAN	Universidad. Panama.
UPRAG/A	Asomante. San Juan, PR, USA. Asociación de graduados de la Universidad de Puerto Rico.
UV/PH	La Palabra y el Hombre. Revista de la Universidad Veracruzana. Xalapa, Mexico.